'I COUNTED THEM
ALL OUT AND
I COUNTED THEM
ALL BACK'

BRIAN HANRAHAN AND ROBERT FOX

'I COUNTED THEM ALL OUT AND I COUNTED THEM ALL BACK'

THE BATTLE FOR THE FALKLANDS

BRITISH BROADCASTING CORPORATION

All the dispatches and interviews in this book were recorded for use in BBC News programmes. Some TV News commentaries are also included. The pictures that accompanied them often reached London two or three weeks after the event. No satellite facilities were available to the TV correspondents with the Task Force; their tapes and films had to be shipped by mail bag.

Robert Fox's *Listener* articles at the end of the book were specially commissioned, and our thanks are due to the Editor of *The Listener* for permission to reprint them.

The book was compiled and edited by John Heuston, Editor, Information and Research, BBC, who also wrote the linking pieces.

A video cassette based on the BBC television series *Task Force South* will be available from retailers from mid-August, or direct from BBC Video, PO Box 356, Ealing, London W5 2YH.

Published by the British Broadcasting Corporation,
35 Marylebone High Street, London W1M 4AA

ISBN 0 563 20147 9
First published 1982
Reprinted 1982
© British Broadcasting Corporation 1982

Set in 9/10 Times by Yale Press, London SE25 5LY
and printed in England by Cox & Wyman Limited, Reading
Cover and photographs printed by Belmont Press Limited,
Northampton

CONTENTS

Foreword	7
The Voyage Out	9
Air Battles	19
First Landings	33
Goose Green and Darwin	43
Bluff Cove	69
Surrender of Port Stanley	75
In Memoriam	89
The Communications War	93
Looking Back from London	99
Chronology	135
About the Authors	138

FOREWORD

'I counted them all out and I counted them all back.' Brian Hanrahan found a memorable phrase to assure anxious listeners of the safe return of the Harriers to HMS *Hermes* after their first attack on the landing strip of Port Stanley. They were words that echoed around the world, widely quoted as a statement of plain truth. Truth is the only counter to propaganda.

The broadcasts by the two BBC special correspondents with the Task Force, Brian Hanrahan and Robert Fox, will remain in people's memories of the Falklands campaign of 2 April – 15 June 1982. Many viewers and listeners have sought a more permanent record of their reports. This book is that record.

Alan Protheroe
Assistant Director General BBC

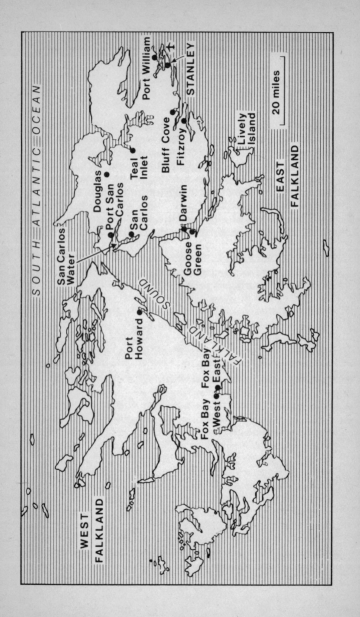

THE VOYAGE OUT

Like everyone else who sailed with the Task Force, Brian Hanrahan and Robert Fox set out hurriedly with not much warning and no certainty of how the voyage would end.

Brian Hanrahan was just back from leave, helping the office out over the busy weekend that followed the Argentine invasion of the Falklands on Friday 2 April. 'You've just had a sailing holiday,' said his Editor. 'How about another one?' By Monday he had left Portsmouth on the *Hermes* with his camera team, Bernard Hesketh and John Jockel.

Robert Fox left Southampton on board the *Canberra* four days later thinking it might all be 'long and boring with no action'. He had been awarded a Churchill Fellowship and had arranged to be in Newfoundland studying local radio in a few weeks' time. Ironically, he was to find a very similar small-community radio system in the Falklands.

At first sight, the luxury liner *Canberra* seemed a better billet than the elderly aircraft-carrier *Hermes*. But Fox found himself sharing a tiny cabin, and the food was not normal P & O cruise fare. At least he could sometimes get through to London on the ship's telephone. Hanrahan was already experiencing the acute communications difficulties fully described later in the book. As the *Hermes* maintained radio silence, he had to hitch helicopter rides to smaller ships to file his dispatches. The entry in his journal for one Monday reads: 'Made it to *Olmeda* just before the Nine O' Clock News . . . Wait until midnight to get dispatch away. Then got stuck on *Olmeda* until Wednesday because weather too bad to fly. Dispatch not sent . . .'

For the earlier part of the voyage the Haig mission was in progress and prospects of a diplomatic solution seemed hopeful. By the end of April, as the Task Force approached the Falklands in worsening weather, the daily routine of drills and exercises had become a preparation for almost inevitable war.

THE *HERMES* LEAVES PORTSMOUTH

Brian Hanrahan: Monday 5 April 1982

We departed with gentle punctuality. Promptly at 10.45 the ship nudged out from the quay; at first so slowly it was hardly noticeable.

Long naval tradition brought the ship's company to the rails in their best uniforms – among them the green berets of the Royal Marines brought aboard to be part of any landing force. The Sea King helicopters and Harrier jets were drawn up on deck – a display of the ship's strength.

For hours past sailors and marines had swayed aboard ton after ton of ammunition, but now the breakneck activity was over. There'll be a long pause while the Task Force steams to the other end of the world.

The *Invincible*, Britain's other carrier, steamed out ahead of us – swapping signals with our flag-deck from where the fleet will be controlled. We followed out into the Solent. Crowds waved us away from every vantage point.

The ship's company lined the sides to exchange salutes – courtesies were swapped with HMS *Victory*, Nelson's old flagship, still a commissioned ship for the Royal Navy. But this fleet which the Government has warned it's willing to use in anger is by far the most powerful the Royal Navy has ever put to sea.

DRILLS AND EXERCISES

Brian Hanrahan: Tuesday 6 April

Hermes has been exercising extensively all morning. Flying stations were piped immediately after breakfast and since then the Harrier jets and the Sea King helicopters have bobbed and weaved around the carrier as their crews recovered their skills. The captain of *Hermes* is Captain Lin Middleton – his son is a helicopter pilot with another ship on the force. Once the planes were airborne the captain sent all hands to action stations. A routine-enough drill, but one this voyage invests with deadly significance.

All of us have been asked to wear anti-flash masks during action stations. They are cumbersome and uncomfortable but they'll be vital if there's real danger of attack. And we've also been warned that all beards will have to be shaved off, in order to make gas masks fit properly. There was one break from flying today, to give the Royal Marines time to exercise. But with all the below-deck space full of men, machinery and ammunition, they have to use the flight-deck, so for an hour each day even the precious flying time is given up to keep the Marines fit to fight.

FLYING IN A 'JUNGLY'

Brian Hanrahan: Saturday 10 April

We went flying from *Hermes* in a 'jungly', that's the Navy's name for the green camouflaged troop-carrying helicopters. From the skies we watched the *Invincible*, the other carrier in our Task Force, manoeuvring with two of the frigate escorts, their wakes cutting pale-blue paths through the deeper colours of the undisturbed ocean. They were battling with each other, training their guns across the divide and every weapon on the Harriers that screamed in low over the horizon, simulating attacks.

We winched down to both frigates; aboard, their exercises were for flood, fire, almost every sort of damage. And there was considerable humour. We saw a cartoon with the names of the ships in our part of the force – names I can't give for fear of jeopardising naval security – and below is the caption, 'The Empire strikes back'. And one group said they'd already booked a dance hall for the night they landed in Port Stanley. 'Come along,' they said confidently, 'you're all invited.'

11

THE *HERMES* GETS ORGANISED

Brian Hanrahan: Sunday 11 April
Shown on TV News 17 April

HMS *Hermes* put to sea in haste. Her crew were straggling back from leave as hundreds of tons of stores piled aboard. The first hours were crazy ones, tidying up people and equipment and then buckling down to building a fighting ship. The Navy has boarded every Harrier it had and scoured its ground stations for the pilots to fly them. Skilled combat pilots though they were, they needed first to recover the skill of operating from a moving deck at sea.

The exercise also let the squadron into the ship's system. They meet through the flight-deck officer. Lightly clad in a yellow jacket, he marshals the aircraft, trying to keep planes and people apart, Harriers and helicopters airborne simultaneously. Drills day and night sharpen reactions, squeezing minutes off the response time. The damage-control centre, HQ1, monitors the time taken to seal up the ship against attack. Experienced petty officers instruct young seamen in the unchanging routine of shoring up bulkheads against leaks. 'Good defence', we were told, ' can save the ship, even if it is hit.'

As the ship turns steadily south, a bustling island on an empty sea, the crew becomes more thoughtful. The news reaching us from home suggests that war is becoming thinkable, that *Hermes*, the flagship of the fleet, will be a primary target. There's a real chance that all this drill and practice will be needed. This is no longer a game.

THE *CANBERRA*: LUXURY LINER TURNED TROOPSHIP

Robert Fox: *From Our Own Correspondent*
Monday 12 April

After a weekend of the grey swell of the Western Approaches to the British Isles, the 45,000-ton luxury-cruise liner is now ploughing through calmer and sunnier waters. After a peaceful Easter Sunday the troops are getting down to a heavy week of training and instruction in stripping and assembling weapons, machine-guns and rifles, and specialist training with anti-tank guns and missiles and mortars. The marines and paratroopers are now constructing the rifle range at the ship's stern for target practice with live ammunition. Morale is high and the troops have settled quickly to their new surroundings, the most luxurious for any land units in the Task Force.

Canberra, whose crest displays proudly her strong Australian ties, would normally take passengers on world or Mediterranean cruises. Now it's a far from relaxed routine for her present company, which includes fifteen women employees of the P & O Line. Morning and evening there is the thunder of marines running in army boots round the decks as the incessant routine of personal fitness training goes on. The *Canberra* has had a considerable facelift above decks, and not one that has made her necessarily more beautiful. Two helicopter pads have been fitted for transferring troops by Sea King helicopters; fittings have been added to enable refuelling at sea from naval tankers. This has attracted the attention of a Russian intelligence-gathering vessel. As *Canberra* practised firing lines to the tanker *Plumleaf*, the spy ship closed to under two miles, photographing anyone and everything on the liner's decks. The spray of aerials from the Russian vessel suggested that she was more interested in the radio and signal traffic with London and the rest of the fleet.

There are moments of peculiar Englishness. In the bar two aristocratic cavalry officers were overheard lamenting the opening of the polo season and the other was more worried about whether his bronze sculpture would be accepted for the Royal Academy summer exhibition than almost anything that might or might not await them in the Falkland Islands.

On Easter Sunday, an extravagant woodcarving of an elephant mascot of a Royal Marines unit was proudly carried into the temporary officers' mess and wardroom, accompanied by a Marines band. An officer from another unit said, 'Whatever else happens on this trip, that thing can't be guaranteed a safe passage.' And shortly afterwards I saw the strangest sight of all – a Marine bandsman going into the ladies' lavatory with a violin under his arm.

A few minutes later there were the unmistakable sounds of a Bach practice piece. Because there are so few women aboard, the ladies' lavatory has now become officially the bandroom of the Royal Marines musicians, who double as stretcher-bearers in battle conditions.

CANBERRA IN FREETOWN
Robert Fox: Sunday 18 April

None of the 2000 troops aboard was allowed ashore. There were a few well-wishers on shore, waving Union Jacks and shouting 'Good Luck' from speedboats in the harbour. Men in bumboats offered skins and ornaments, but the marines and paratroopers were told of the risk of bringing anthrax aboard if they bought animal skins.

The ship was visited by the British High Commissioner in Freetown, Mr Terence O'Leery. The twenty-six dock-yard men from Vosper Thorneycroft went ashore; they completed the second flight-deck for helicopters on the *Canberra* before the weekend. A signal from *Canberra* to the men's employers praised them for working tirelessly in difficult and stormy conditions. 'The enthusiasm and sheer hard work of these men', said the signal, 'is greatly appreciated.'

AN ARGENTINE PLANE
Brian Hanrahan: Wednesday 21 April

One of the Harriers from *Hermes* was scrambled to intercept, and reported that the plane was an Argentine Boeing 707 in military colours, all white with blue and white roundels and flags. The Argentine air force has one military Boeing used for troop-carrying and reconnaissance. It's their longest-range aircraft and is thought to be unarmed. Although the Harrier had live missiles, the pilot who intercepted was under orders not to fire except in self-defence. With the *Hermes* Harrier in close company, the Boeing flew around the fleet at high altitude. It came within twelve miles before heading back to Argentina. The Argentine plane came straight towards the fleet at a steady bearing – an unlikely coincidence in the vast Southern Ocean, unless it already knew where we were.

The *Hermes* is now 2500 miles from the Falklands, and expects to be within range of attack by Friday. From then on, the ship will be at permanent defence watches.

MAJOR NORMAN RETURNS
Robert Fox: Sunday 25 April

The members of the Falklands naval party who defended Port Stanley arrived here by air. After a few days' leave they volunteered to join the forces that are preparing for any assault on the Falklands. As they posed for photographs on heaps of ammunition boxes on the aft sundeck of the *Canberra*, Major Mike Norman produced a Falklands flag, acquired there by another officer several years ago. The flag, a Union Jack with the sheep and galleon crest on a red ground, bears the motto: 'Desire the Right'. Major Norman says he has every intention of seeing that this flag flies over Government House at Port Stanley when his Royal Marines return. Though many of his men were only four days into their commission on the island, they have been able to provide valuable information about the troops and weapons the Argentines are deploying there.

Thorough briefings are being given to specialist forces that might go ashore to prepare a landing, the reconnaissance and surveillance patrols and the Arctic and mountain-warfare units. A roll is being taken of any soldiers who can ride, as they will be asked to help round up the hundreds of thousands of sheep now thought to be on the loose in the remoter outlands. Some of the most valuable local information is being given by an officer [Major Ewan Southby Taylour] who has been preparing a book about the island. A couple of months ago his publishers said they

15

might not print the book after all. They told him they doubted that anyone would be interested in a book on the Falklands nowadays.

SOUTH GEORGIA RECAPTURED

Brian Hanrahan: Sunday 25 April

The Argentinians surrendered before the main British force went ashore. They'd been softened up by the advance party, a naval bombardment, and the disabling of an Argentine submarine.

The submarine, the *Santa Fe*, had been detected making its way to South Georgia in a blizzard. Royal Navy helicopters attacked with torpedoes and depth charges. It limped away disabled – listing and discharging smoke and diesel oil. It ran aground in a bay to the north of the island close to an old whaling station at Grytvyken. The reports from the attacking British ships, HMS *Antrim* and *Endurance*, indicate that it had severe internal damage and cannot dive. A few hours after a naval bombardment the helicopters swept into action again carrying troops from the Task Force ashore. Another wave of Royal Marine commandos trained in Arctic warfare waited to move in but they weren't needed. The Argentine troops holding Grytvyken raised the white flag. So far there's no report of the numbers involved on either side or if casualties were suffered.

The victory signal was sent to London: 'Be pleased to inform Her Majesty that the White Ensign flies alongside the Union Flag at Grytvyken, South Georgia.'

South Georgia is 800 miles from the Falkland Island group and is administered from Port Stanley. The latest troubles began there when Argentine scrap-metal merchants arrived to dismantle an old whaling station. It's uninhabited except for an outpost of the British Antarctic Survey. South Georgia's importance to the Task Force is more than psychological. It's a land base close to the scene of operations – a foothold which can be expanded.

ADMIRAL'S REACTIONS

Brian Hanrahan: Tuesday 27 April

Admiral Woodward said he'd been surprised how quickly the opposition had surrendered. 'We were led to believe they were a tough lot but they soon threw in their hand when 4½-inch shells started wanging about them.' They could expect a repeat performance in the Falklands.

The success of the South Georgia operation had been a tremendous boost for his men, the Admiral said. Early success was always heart-warming. He now had a secure base with sheltered waters out of reach of the Argentine air force. Store ships, hospital ships could ride out the Antarctic storms, warships could even carry out repairs. Not as good as a Royal Dockyard, he said, but a considerable asset.

We are now well advanced into the Roaring Forties, the strong winds whipping up the grey waters; the temperature's falling daily. From his seat below the bridge, Admiral Woodward looking out at the full Task Force formed up around him and said: 'This is the heavy punch. As we get closer the options become fewer. The sands are running out.' And he finished with a warning to the Argentine troops on the Falklands. 'If you want to get out I suggest you do so now. Once we arrive the only way home will be courtesy of the Royal Navy.'

AIR BATTLES

On 30 April, ten days after the final breakdown of Secretary of State Haig's mediation efforts between London and Buenos Aires, the United States came out openly on Britain's side. The United Nations became the centre of attempts at a diplomatic solution, but though talks dragged on for three more weeks, no real common ground was established.

On HMS *Hermes* Brian Hanrahan witnessed final preparations for the first air attacks on Port Stanley. On the evening of 30 April he heard the Captain broadcast to the ship: 'Tomorrow's the big day.' Next morning the Harriers took off and Hanrahan relieved much anxiety with his famous phrase: 'I counted them all out and I counted them all back.' Reconnaissance photographs showed Argentine aircraft damaged at Port Stanley and the airfield cratered, though it was found later that the raid did not finally close Stanley as a base for incoming aircraft.

Next day the Argentine cruiser *General Belgrano* was torpedoed and sunk by a British submarine with the loss of over 300 lives. The Argentines struck back with their fatal Exocet missile attack on HMS *Sheffield*. Robert Fox on the *Canberra* reported that her officers were amazed that a missile from an aircraft could do so much damage. The *Hermes* was near enough to take on board survivors from the *Sheffield*. Her Captain gave a moving account of the desperate fight to save his ship. Eventually, after many times of asking, permission was given for cameraman Bernard Hesketh to fly over the abandoned destroyer before she finally sank.

In Robert Fox's words there was 'apprehension about a long and difficult campaign ahead'. He watched, on the decks of the *Canberra*, repeated embarkation routines for troops preparing for an assault landing. Argentine air attacks on British ships became fiercer and more frequent . . .

'AND I COUNTED THEM ALL BACK'

Brian Hanrahan: Saturday 1 May

At 6 pm on Saturday evening, ships of the Royal Navy went into action off the Falkland Islands. They bombarded the coast with their 4½-inch guns, a follow-up to the morning's bombing runs. As the ships moved in, Mirage fighters of the Argentine Air Force moved out to attack. The Sea Harriers, which had been continually patrolling overhead, swooped to intercept. The planes cartwheeled across the sky in a fierce dogfight. At the end two Argentine planes had been shot down; others were believed to have been damaged. Captain Lin Middleton of HMS *Hermes* said the British aircraft had all returned safely, their pilots uninjured. This was the end of a day in which the Task Force defences had been probed continually by Argentine aircraft. But until the naval bombardment started, each time the aircraft had turned away.

The naval Task Force had entered the exclusion zone around the Falklands at 7 am Greenwich Mean Time in the morning. Within an hour, the air strike had begun. HMS *Hermes*, on its radar, tracked a Vulcan bomber in to shed its load of twenty-one 1000-pound bombs across Stanley airport. The night was an ideal one for surprise: dark and overcast, no moon, just an occasional star breaking through the clouds. As the big bomber turned back to base, we monitored its radio codeword: the mission was successful.

A few hours after the Vulcan attack, it was *Hermes'* turn. At dawn the Navy's Sea Harriers took off, each carrying three 1000-pound bombs. They wheeled in the sky before heading for the islands – at that stage just ninety miles away. Some of the planes went to create more havoc at Stanley, the others to a small airstrip called Goose Green, near Darwin, 120 miles to the west. There they found and bombed a number of grounded aircraft mixed in with decoys. At Stanley the planes went in low, in waves just seconds apart. They glimpsed the bomb craters left by the Vulcan and they left behind them more fire and destruction. The pilots said there had been smoke and dust everywhere, punctuated by the flash of explosions. They faced a barrage of return fire, heavy but apparently ineffective. I'm not allowed to say how many planes joined the raid, but I counted them all out, and I counted them all back. Their pilots were all unhurt, cheerful and jubilant, giving thumbs-up signs. One plane had a single bullet hole through the tail; it's already been repaired.

After studying the reconnaissance photographs, the Admiral's staff pronounced both raids a success – aircraft had been damaged and the airfields cratered. The intention of the attack was threefold: to damage radar and missiles that could threaten the Harriers; to deny Stanley as a base to Argentine aircraft; and to cut off the Falklands by air, enforcing Britain's blockade of the islands. The bombing pattern was designed to strike only at the airport, not at the town which is several miles away. There were intended to be no civilian casualties. At the end of the day Rear-Admiral Sandy Woodward, the Task Force Commander, said: 'We didn't want this fight. I'd hoped we could put it off, but we've shown our colours and it's been our day.'

CANBERRA HEARS OF THE AIR BATTLES
Robert Fox: Sunday 2 May

As the news of the air battles reached the *Canberra*, most of her company were going about their Sunday routine. There was an interdenominational service in the ship's cinema. The conflict with Argentina was hardly mentioned. But a Marine padre did read out a letter from a senior Royal Navy Roman Catholic chaplain in which he mentioned criticism by Cardinal Hume of Argentine aggression.

On the decks embarkation routines were repeated for troops getting into helicopters for an assault landing. News of the fighting has been followed avidly on the BBC's World Service broadcasts, though there has been little sign of outward jubilation. Conversations on the exercise deck take a practical turn: the right clothes for the Falkland climate and the superiority of Royal Marines' close-combat training.

In recent days the *Canberra* has been watched closely by a Russian intelligence-gathering ship. She can monitor wireless traffic and shows intense interest in all that the amphibious units have been doing. Security has become noticeably tighter, and any speculation about future movements and operations is now ruled out. Journalists are not allowed by the Ministry of Defence to comment on what might be happening to other elements of the Task Force. 'We don't want to give the Argentines needlessly clues about future movements,' said the senior Royal Navy captain aboard.

SINKING OF THE *BELGRANO*

Brian Hanrahan: Monday 3 May

The cruiser had been operating outside Britain's 200-mile exclusion zone for several days. At eight o'clock last night a nuclear-powered submarine torpedoed it. It hasn't been sunk, but it has been damaged. The attack was selective – the cruiser's escorts were allowed to escape. The *General Belgrano* was an old World War II cruiser; it had fifteen big guns and a crew of more than a thousand to man them. Despite its fire-power, it was perhaps the least worrying of the serious threats to the Task Force. Because of its age it would make a great deal of noise in the water, an easy trace for Britain's nuclear hunter-killer submarines which have been on station here for some time.

The overnight skirmish began when a Sea King helicopter came across an Argentine patrol boat, a converted tug armed with a machine-gun. The tug opened fire on the Sea King, which called in reinforcements. A Lynx helicopter armed with the latest radar-guided missile, the Sea Skua, attacked the target and sank it. *Hermes* called in another helicopter to search for survivors, but as it approached it was fired on by another Argentine patrol boat. The Lynx attacked the second patrol boat with missiles and damaged it. By this time it was running short of fuel and had to abandon the search.

The Task Force has now dealt heavy blows at both the

Argentine Navy and the Air Force, as well as bombing and damaging the airport at Port Stanley. So far it's shown that it can enforce the sea and air blockade of the islands that Admiral Woodward, the Commander, said he intended to establish.

LOSS OF THE *SHEFFIELD*

Brian Hanrahan: Tuesday 4 May

The British Task Force has lost a Type 42 destroyer, HMS *Sheffield*, in an Argentine air attack. A British Sea Harrier was shot down during a bombing mission over the Falklands.

The attack was made by a low-flying aircraft slipping in beneath the Fleet's guard. They launched a missile that hit HMS *Sheffield*, a guided-missile destroyer, causing some casualties and much damage. The number of casualties isn't yet known. The survivors are still being counted. But the first indications are that nearly all of the crew of about 300 men were saved.

Sheffield was on the edge of our defensive screen. From the deck of HMS *Hermes*, the flagship, I could see a pillar of white smoke on the horizon, which continued to climb until dark and the decision was made to abandon her. Throughout the afternoon a shuttle of helicopters moved between us – taking doctors and fire-fighting equipment to *Sheffield*; bringing the injured back here – a few on stretchers, but most, though obviously dazed, were able to walk with somebody's shoulder for support.

When it became obvious the fire couldn't be controlled the crew abandoned ship. The sea was gentle to them; mild with a long smooth swell. The wild weather of recent days would have made rescue more hazardous. As it was, everybody who left the ship was picked up. The survivors are being transferred to *Hermes* which has more space to accommodate them. A reception area has been set up to supply bedding and clothes; doctors and the chaplain are on hand.

CANBERRA HEARS OF THE *SHEFFIELD*

Robert Fox: Tuesday 4 May

The news came at suppertime in the evening. Waiters serving in one of the main dining-rooms had heard the BBC World Service news announcement that the *Sheffield* had been set on fire and was thought to have sunk. Many of the officers I spoke to are amazed that a missile from an aircraft could do such apparent damage.

News bulletins are awaited keenly for further details. Senior officers have said that the Navy and the Fleet Air Arm must control the waters and skies around the Falklands for a successful landing on the islands without numerous casualties. Throughout the day the reports of the debate in Parliament and announcements from the Ministry of Defence have been listened to with intense concentration. Their content is relayed around the ship. The fact that the Argentine forces have sunk a modern destroyer, and shot down a Sea Harrier, has led to apprehension about a long and difficult campaign ahead.

SHEFFIELD SURVIVORS: INTERVIEW WITH CAPTAIN SALT

Brian Hanrahan: Wednesday 5 May
Shown on TV News 26 May

A trickle of *Sheffield* crewmen continue to come aboard the flagship with minor injuries. They were dazed but walking from the helicopters with the assistance of the medical orderlies. After five hours the ship was abandoned to the fire. But *Sheffield* would not sink. After the fire had burned out she was still there, shrouded in sea mist, floating upright. Occasional whisps of steam came from the foredeck where the survivors had gathered waiting to be rescued and singing, 'You've got to look on the bright side of life.' After five hours the captain made the painful decision to abandon ship.

CAPTAIN JOHN SALT: I can tell you that we're talking about

24

seconds to react rather than minutes and I hope, I'm sure, that you'll appreciate that a missile which comes in less than twelve feet off the deck at a very high speed, at hundreds of miles an hour, gives us a very short time of response.

HANRAHAN: How much effect did it have?

SALT: Devastating. It hit the centre of the ship, which is the centre of all operations both mechanical and detection and weapons' systems-wise, about six feet above the water level, damaged two large compartments, and when inside the ship exploded and exploded outwards and upwards. We're actually talking about fifteen to twenty seconds. I know it sounds incredible, but it was fifteen to twenty seconds before the whole of the working area of the ship, and I'm talking about one third of the ship, the centre portion, was filled with black, acrid, pungent smoke.

HANRAHAN: Coming from where?

SALT: Mainly from electrical-cable runs and paint initially. Then, of course, it caught the fuel and all the other combustibles, and when you reach a certain temperature even the hull itself will sustain heat and transmit heat to other parts of the hull, which then spread the fire in a way which is really very dangerous. So initially I would say it was almost certainly cable runs which lost us complete power, electrical lighting, main broadcasts throughout the ship. Within two to three minutes I would say.

HANRAHAN: Could you describe in your own words what happened the minute after . . . how the men reacted, how you reacted?

SALT: Quite incredible. I think we were extremely fortunate that *Sheffield* has been at sea, away from the UK, since the seventeenth of November, which may sound a long time. We were actually due to go back at the beginning of April, but we were diverted for this emergency. And there are some positive sides to that. Really that the ship's company get to know each other. We knock off all our round corners, square corners. Morale was really at an incredibly high level and teamwork was really excellent. That was my overriding impression throughout the five hours that we tried to fight this damage.

HANRAHAN: Five hours?

SALT: Five hours through which we tried to fight the damage. My impression was of immense calm, common sense and careful thinking by really every member of the ship's company.

HANRAHAN: How were you able to go about fighting the damage? You had your power knocked out, and had your command signalling knocked out. How were you able to do that?

SALT: We weren't. Initially our biggest problem was the smoke, the type of smoke which you cannot possibly breath in, and the fact that our fire-fighting water system was completely cut off. We had no power pressure, no fire-main pressure with which to fight the fire, and we could not get below decks anywhere near the scene of damage, which was fairly extensive within two minutes of hitting.

HANRAHAN: And you knew there were men down there?

SALT: Yes, but we didn't know how many. And this I think is where we were fortunate in having been together as a team for so long, and I have no doubt that the ship's company really saved themselves largely by their own sensible efforts. They were quite remarkable.

HANRAHAN: Can you explain to a layman how it was that this could have happened in a battle group of this size with the expertise available to us?

SALT: No, I don't think so at the moment, it's not a subject that I think I have sufficient knowledge about at the moment. But obviously within the group they are passing over our experience to ensure that all can be done possible to minimise this sort of thing happening again. But then you're talking about missile weapons-systems at very high speed and very low height and radar horizons, and how they get affected by height and all the other considerations which go into detection and then reaction, you are thinking about very, very short reaction time. It is a function of the modern missile war.

HANRAHAN: The other ships came to your rescue, of course; we saw the helicopters flying to you.

SALT: Yes, we had some excellent assistance in so far as they were able to provide help from ships and helicopters, but unfortunately their capabilities were unable to allow us to gain on the rate of expansion of the fire.

HANRAHAN: What was it that finally made you decide to give up that fight, to abandon the ship?

SALT: I think I started thinking that we were on a losing wicket when we realised that the fire was spreading. The decks were hot. On the upper deck you could feel the heat of the deck through your feet with shoes on. The super-structure was steaming. The paint on the ship's side was coming off. Around the initial area where the missile penetrated the hull was glowing red, it was white hot and red hot. The flames we could see coming out of the hole. The extent of damage was such that we knew there was no way in that class of ship that you could possibly fight that ship again with that amount of damage.

HANRAHAN: It would have been useless if you had saved it?

SALT: Even if we had saved it. I went back on board. There is no way that that ship could positively contribute to this group.

HANRAHAN: You went back later by helicopter to see it. Even then you accepted that it may be the right decision to abandon?

SALT: I have no doubt at all, I'm afraid. We went back by

helicopter about seven hours after the explosion, and the whole of the centre section was a roaring mass of flame, that is the whole of the working area of the ship.

HANRAHAN: It was your decision to abandon ship?

SALT: Yes, it was. I'd just like to say that the other part of the decision to abandon was the fact that we were taking the attention of other ships and units in the area at a time when we were subject to attack. We had no hope of retrieving the fighting capability of that ship. The fire had extended to an extent that was dangerous with regard to our own ammunition magazines, missile magazines, and the ship's company, all of them, were on the upper deck and had been on the upper deck in very cold conditions for five hours. We were not winning that fire, beating it, we were losing.

DEATH OF THE *SHEFFIELD*
Brian Hanrahan: Monday 10 May

The Task Force has been back in action off the Falklands, harassing the islands' defenders by sea and air. Under cover of darkness last night, ships moved in close to the islands to bombard military installations. But there was no attempted landing, as the Argentines have claimed. It was part of the continuous softening-up process to prepare for an eventual invasion by British forces. The Sea Harriers cruised above, dropping occasional flares to see what was happening. On one occasion they surprised a Hercules transport plane being escorted to Port Stanley by Mirage fighters. The fighters turned away without engaging the Harriers and the transport turned back to the mainland.

This morning an Argentine trawler was sighted by one of the Harriers well inside the exclusion zone, to the south-east of the islands. The pilot recognised it as the *Narwhal*, an ocean-going trawler which had already been warned by a British frigate to leave the area a week ago. He strafed it and the last report said it had stopped dead in the water. The vessel's persistence in returning to the area indicates it may be serving a military purpose.

Certainly for the past few days some Argentine air and sea traffic has been getting to the Falklands, probably bringing in stores. They have gone unchallenged because a thick sea mist had made it dangerous for the Harriers to operate. With visibility down to 700 yards, their chances of finding the carriers once they had taken off would have been low. Now that three Harriers from the limited number have been lost, it was a risk considered only worth running if the Task Force itself was under attack. But as the skies cleared the pressure on the Argentine forces occupying the Falklands was restored.

The Navy made every effort to save HMS *Sheffield*. One of the other ships of the Task Force managed to get a line aboard and tow it out of the exclusion zone, where she was handed over to an ocean-going tug. The fires aboard were under control or out. But the sea roughened, water poured into the huge hole on the starboard side where the missile had struck, and the crew of the tug had to cut the towline and then watch her sink.

Before this happened she had made an eerie sight drifting in and out of the mist banks, steam still rising from hatches on the foredeck. Around the hole were black patches where the paint was blistered off by the fire within. The radar domes on the upper deck were burnt and twisted by the heat, the helicopter hangar on the stern full of ash.

Salvaging *Sheffield* would have been more than a matter of pride for the Navy. It would have yielded invaluable information about the strengths and weaknesses of modern ships. The lessons from *Sheffield* are already being applied aboard *Hermes*. Principally that involves keeping all doors and hatches closed to prevent the spread of smoke and fire if there's a hit.

Generally, there is immense relief here that Nimrod reconnaissance aircraft have been dispatched to give the fleet airborne radar cover. It has been realised that the Navy was vulnerable to low-flying aircraft slipping in below radar. The attack on the *Sheffield* showed how dangerous that weakness was, especially on a calm sea.

PROBING THE DEFENCES

Brian Hanrahan: Tuesday 11 May

A warship from what's known as a Surface Action Group
left the Task Force and went close in to the Falklands this
morning. There it identified an Argentine resupply vessel
just after one o'clock in the morning, London time. The
supply vessel was fired on by the ship, and an explosion
was heard in its vicinity. There are, however, no details of
what damage was done, or what happened to the ship.

It's believed that this happened in the sound between
the two islands, and it is an example of the way in which
Britain is spreading its blockade steadily around the
Falklands. We have now been told of a story of a frigate
which two days ago passed right around the island and
down the sound between them. It went along looking in
every bay and harbour it could find, making as much noise
as possible, deliberately putting itself close to the west
coast of the island, rather than enforcing the blockade on
the east coast. It fired its guns, it put up a helicopter, it
dropped a flare. But it found no sign of life in any harbour.
It saw no movement on any jetty, it was not opposed by
any forces. It was as though the opposition had refused to
take up this deliberate challenge.

CHANGES ON BOARD *HERMES*

Brian Hanrahan: Tuesday 11 May

When HMS *Hermes* steamed from Portsmouth, her officers dined in traditional normal splendour. They wore
cummerbunds and evening dress, sat at tables laid with a
silver service, and ate by the light of candelabra.

Now these tables are frequently overturned in the
middle of the floor, tied firmly down by thick rope, the
chairs locked on top like barricades in a Belfast street.
Around them men in grubby overalls eat snack meals,
taking ten minutes away from their action stations. At
their waist the highly-coloured cummerbunds have given
way to blue webbing belts. On each is clipped a gas mask,

a life jacket and a survival suit – an all-embracing garment made of dayglo orange rubber. It looks like a pair of baggy pyjamas, but wearing it in the chilly waters of the South Atlantic increases survival time from minutes to hours.

Like the men, the ship is wound up tight. Every watertight door is closed and walking around the ship means constantly knocking off the metal clips which hold the doors in place and ramming them back after passing through. To pass from one deck to another means scrambling through tiny manholes, twisting and turning to get through with all the survival kit at your waist: groping for the heavy metal hatch to bolt it down over your head. Each hatch is marked with a Z, the last letter of the alphabet. This is condition Z alert, the Navy's highest level of preparedness.

Some of the hatches used to be left open, but since the disaster of the *Sheffield*, when fire and smoke spread within seconds, they're all closed and nobody complains. But although the ship can be kept sealed up, men can't. Normally the ship stays at defence watches, moving up to action stations only when there's considered a high threat of attack. Defence watches are quite hard enough. Every position on board is manned, the crew do six hours on and six off, and they sleep in their clothes ready to rush into position if the alarm sounds. With the ship sealed up against attack, nobody is allowed to sleep below the waterline, so on the upper deck there's a system of 'hot bunking', one man taking over a bed as another leaves it. It isn't to all tastes and some of the crew have been bringing their mattresses up to sleep near their action stations. More than one senior officer with a long memory has been bewailing the phasing out of hammocks from the Navy.

The call to action stations is a klaxon – a routine-enough sound in peacetime exercises, a chilling one in war. For minutes there's frantic activity as the off-watch rushes into position, slamming closed the hatches behind them, pulling on their anti-flash gloves and masks, the white material growing grubbier with frequent use. Then the ship settles into a tense stillness, braced for attack. In the long corridors nobody moves, it could be a ghost ship.

On the bridge the intercoms chatter, but if they have to do anything up here it will be too late. In a modern missile war the ship fights from the operations room, surrounded by the orange flicker of radar. *Star Wars* tempered by Jack Hawkins accents. The incongruous sound is the old-fashioned ring of the telephone – 1950s' model. Outside in the mist the aircrew wait to launch the Harriers. It could be a still life.

Most times it is; the alarm passes uneventfully. So far I've not seen an enemy, but I've been aware of every hostile aircraft for – well, security doesn't allow me to say how many miles. It's a nerve-wracking business, especially since *Sheffield* blew up on our horizon, demonstrating how real the danger is.

Some of the younger sailors will admit quite frankly that they're scared. Perhaps they have more courage than those who don't. It isn't easy living inside the vulnerable metal skin of a ship, breathing artificial air, seeing nothing but artificial light. Now the flight-deck is always at battle readiness there are few chances to see the outside world for real.

But each heightened state of readiness is greeted with relief rather than regret, despite the extra inconvenience. Not that there aren't grumbles. Each time action stations are called all loose objects are put away, and in the petty officers' mess a lot of unfinished pints of beer a day are going down the drain. With a ration of two pints a day that's a serious business. In the Navy they call such grumbling 'dripping' – and they say as long as a sailor drips there isn't much wrong with him.

FIRST LANDINGS

On 14 May Brian Hanrahan saw the night sky light up as commandos destroyed Argentine aircraft in a raid on Pebble Island, off the north coast of West Falkland. A week later came the main British landing at San Carlos Bay in East Falkland. Robert Fox was one of the first two British correspondents to go ashore with the Paras. On the way he endured the frightening experience of 'the galley port leap', as he jumped from the ferry *Norland* into a landing craft. One paratrooper fell between ship and landing craft, crushing his pelvis. A day or two later Brian Hanrahan's feet touched the Falklands for the first time. 'I jumped up and down and picked heather.'

For the first week after the landings the British ships in 'bomb alley' endured strong and determined Argentine air attacks. There was more tragic loss of life as the *Ardent*, *Antelope* and others were destroyed.

On 25 May the Argentines again used the French missile Exocet to deadly effect. The *Atlantic Conveyor* was irreparably damaged and went down, taking with her the 'heavy-lift' helicopters needed for the final assault on Port Stanley.

COMMANDO RAID
Brian Hanrahan: Sunday 16 May

Fifty commandos went ashore – they landed on Pebble
Island, the northernmost part of the Falklands, where
Argentina had set up an air-base. They touched down
some miles away from the target and took several hours to
reach it across rugged country in the dark. Then, in the
dead of night, the battle exploded in front of me, as I
watched from a destroyer just offshore. The bulk of the
island black against a luminous sky was suddenly lit up by
star shells and red tracer lines, which climbed lazily up
towards the Argentine positions. From the sea the ships
threw out orange flame and covering fire. First, more star
shells to show the attacking force on the ground, then
salvo after salvo of high explosives, each whining away
into the darkness to land on the defenders – twenty at a
time, one shell every two seconds – a tempo designed to
terrify as much as destroy.

The barrage was controlled by a Royal Artillery spot-
ter, ashore on an overlooking hillside. With his calm voice
coming across the radio net, the ship steadily moved its
aim closer to the Argentine positions. The commandos
followed, destroying parked aircraft as they went. The
ship reverberated as the guns kept firing; the muzzle
flashes silhouetted the look-outs, the wind picking at their
Arctic clothing while they stared towards the shore. With
so much man-made brilliance, a shooting star went
through the Southern Cross unremarked.

The barrage was halted to avoid dropping shells close
to Pebble Island settlement, a hamlet of about fifty
people, grouped along the shore in one of the bays. In the
sudden silence we could see, but not hear, the continuing
firefight flickering along the shoreline; but nobody tried to
fire back at us.

The ship's part finished, we turned away from the gun
lines, speeding out from the rear of the island into a force
nine gale, but back to the shelter of the Task Force before
daylight exposed us to air attack. The last message from
shore said there were four aircraft yet to be destroyed, and
then on the horizon behind us there were three distinct
flashes of very powerful explosions. Later a navy spokes-

man said the commandos had blown up an ammunition dump and destroyed eleven aircraft (six Pucaras, one Skyhawk and four light aircraft). That's more than have been lost in the air so far.

The main purpose of the raid was to tighten the blockade. The airstrip had been receiving stores from the mainland and flying them to other bases in the islands. But the aircraft based there – the Pucaras – are also used for ground attack against troops, so destroying them also minimises the danger when the time comes to invade. There were a hundred shells fired during the raid in little more than thirty minutes; since Britain moved to recapture the Falklands, the Navy has fired a thousand salvoes, making this the most intense period of British bombardment since the Second World War.

ASHORE WITH THE PARAS

Robert Fox: Friday 21 May

The assault force approached the Falklands in ideal conditions. Thick cloud, driving rain and a gale. The night itself was bright and starry and had no moon. I embarked with a Parachute battalion in four landing craft exactly the D-day model; the force approached a sheltered inlet with a hamlet of a few houses and a jetty. Only a few dogs barked. It appeared that surprise was complete. Then the dramatic moment of the ramp going down, and the dash up the beach. Now this is the moment we've been waiting for, the ramp is down. We're going forward.

I'm in the water. And I'm on the beach now. We're going ashore with paratroopers heavily laden with missiles and guns. It's a very quiet night. A starlit night, and now we're ashore. A British parachute force is back on the Falklands . . .

During the landings at different points in the creek and anchorage there was persistent naval bombardment. The night air was thick with cordite. Only one of the units, another paratroop battalion, encountered resistance ashore. They had a brisk fire fight, and there were

Argentine casualties and prisoners. They were brought back to the liner *Canberra* which has a comprehensive hospital. Doctors struggled with rudimentary Spanish to reassure the Argentine wounded, who appeared to be in their teens mostly. Throughout the daylight hours *Canberra* herself has been the target of continuous attacks by aircraft, and the troops digging in on high ground have been watched by unpleasant Pucaras – anti-guerrilla warfare aircraft of the Argentinians. I saw three of these hugging the contours of the hills, as the Paras dug desperately in the peat.

LANDING BY STEALTH

Brian Hanrahan: Saturday 22 May

The landing was carried out by stealth rather than force. The ships moved into the main channel between the Falklands and dropped anchor, safe from the sight of an Argentine garrison only by the dark moonless night. For the next hours the troops clambered down scrambling nets lashed alongside, into the landing craft that shuffled back and forth to the shore. It was an agonisingly long operation – nearly four hours from start to finish. All carried out in total silence, both real silence and radio silence.

I saw the dark bulk of the landing craft move up alongside the ship, guided only by the short stabs of the luminous wand on the deck. It showed only the merest glimpse of navigation lights to mark its place, and the stars just caught the flash of the white ensign fluttering at the stern before it was swallowed up by the darkness. At one point several ships started to bombard the shoreline. Not intensively, but making it look like a repeat of the shelling which has been happening nightly at points round the island. At one time heavy fire broke out ashore when an Argentine garrison resisted one of the landing parties.

ARGENTINE AIR ATTACKS
Brian Hanrahan: Saturday 22 May

It was a brilliantly clear dawn. A beautiful day – a clear one. Clear enough to see the troops climbing up the hillside as they secured the beachhead. Clear enough to see the first settlement to fall back under British control. Thirty-one people, six children now back under the British umbrella; their white cottages tucked into the rolling pastures, where the sheep were grazing. But it was clear, too, for the enemy aircraft that came to find the fleet and attack it.

The air attack started an hour after dawn, and has continued right through the day until now. First came the small Pucara bombers' ground attack. Low and surprising. One of them got right into the bay to drop its bombs, but without success. For a few moments the air was full of missiles, as the defending ships fired back. I saw one Pucara making off over a hill with a missile chasing it. The Captain saw a flash in the sky and debris tumbling down. That set the pattern for the rest of the day. Wave after wave of air attacks came against the fleet. First they had to fight or outwit the Harriers which were between them and the islands. Then they had to go through the Task Force frigates and destroyers, which were deployed to put up a missile stream, but still some of the attacking planes got through to where we were anchored.

This morning, for example, two Mirages came sweeping down across the bay. We didn't see them at first. We saw the red wake of the anti-aircraft missiles rushing out to meet them. Then there was a roar of their engines, the explosion of bombs, missiles, everybody firing together. One stray missile went off in the air about 100 yards away. Two bombs exploded harmlessly in the hilltops as the planes curved away, diving back where they'd come from.

But much of the fighting didn't take place in the bay where we were. It was out in the channel outside. We could see the smoke rising over the hills that cut us off. Three of the ships out there were hit by guns or bombs. Two suffered serious damage. But it's not yet clear what the casualties were. The Argentine forces too were suffering losses. The garrison here was cut off. Some we think

37

were killed, the others surrendered. Then we heard of two Mirages which had been shot down. Then another two, a Pucara, a Skyhawk. Another Skyhawk.

As the day went on, more of the attacks came from the Skyhawk fighter-bombers. In one short period ten or a dozen of them dived down on the ships at anchor, producing the same barrage of fire and counterfire. This time there was a new element. The anti-aircraft batteries on the shore joined in. Slowly a defensive screen was being built over the bay, and the worst period of our vulnerability was over. Throughout the day, beneath the air attacks, the helicopters kept on flying. They stayed below radar range. They left the air above clear for the missiles. But they went on, ferrying in men and machinery and all the equipment that the troops need to build a secure beachhead. They also brought in, most urgently of all, the anti-aircraft batteries that are being built on the shores alongside us to secure the beachhead and make it safe for all the troops to move through in their bid to recapture the Falkland Islands.

MORE SHIPS LOST

Brian Hanrahan: Sunday 23 May
(Shown on TV News 19 June)

After the air attacks on the first day (Friday), all but the most essential ships left the anchorage. We returned at first light on Sunday morning, a small group of store ships with a naval escort, untroubled by the prospects of surface attack but worried about air-raids until we turned in from the Falkland Sound, under the cover of the Rapier anti-aircraft missiles in the hills surrounding San Carlos Bay.

The Bay had been shrewdly chosen, not only to provide calm waters for the unloading but to give the shipping inside the maximum protection from air attack. The hills provided a defensive screen, making direct attack difficult and giving the Argentine pilots only a few seconds to pick their target from the ships spread before them.

The air-raids began on Sunday afternoon, blurring

together in a series of attacks which continued, it seems, for days. As the raiders came in the air filled with missiles and machine-guns. The defensive fire took a heavy toll of Argentine planes. But the British underestimated the willingness of Argentina to keep sending in planes against all the odds, and to keep losing them.

It was inevitable that against such an onslaught there would be British losses. One of them was the frigate *Antelope*. She came limping up the bay making excessive smoke. The main mast was bent over where an Argentine plane had clipped it. It was almost a kamikaze attack and it had succeeded. On each side of the hull there was a hole where a bomb had gone in. She anchored about half a mile away and after dark exploded and caught fire.

Despite the danger of further explosions helicopters were soon overhead searching through the smoke and steam for survivors. There were only a handful of casualties, and once everyone had been recovered the ships and the helicopters withdrew. They left *Antelope* to burn on uncontrollably into the night. At times there were explosions as the armaments grew too hot, sending great cascades of hot debris into the air. For the men on all ships anchored about it was a horrifying sight. At dawn she was still smouldering, the upper decks burnt down to just a framework of mangled metal. Later she sank into the bay beneath a great cloud of white smoke. When it cleared just the bows and the stern were left settling in the water.

HMS *Antelope*, like the other ships to be lost or damaged, was an easy target. A modern navy is not designed for individual ships to withstand concerted air attack. They're part of a fleet meant to operate within air cover and, in going ahead without gaining air control, the navy was certain to suffer losses.

But while the warships were attacked, the heavy equipment was being lifted off and only during the most dangerous moments did the helicopters need to hide amid the green folds of the shoreline. Around the bay the marines and paratroopers were establishing themselves and, by ignoring the constant traffic, the Argentine planes lost the chance to smash the beachhead before it could settle itself.

In one raid I was caught in a helicopter over the bay

and it was our turn to take cover on the hillside. We watched the attack from a rise in the ground, and the attacking Skyhawks turned directly over our helicopter as though they intended to attack. But instead they made off over the top, black trails of Rapier missiles tracing after them. Later we learnt the missiles had caught up with two of the three in the formation. The Rapier crews were improving their accuracy with practice.

The raids continued on the Tuesday, Argentina's Independence Day, and one pilot was shot down directly over HMS *Fearless*, after dropping his bomb. He came down by parachute, his head bobbing in the water a few hundred yards away. An enemy had turned into another human in danger and a boat was sent to pick him up and bring him up in a landing craft through the big open dock at the back of *Fearless*. The medical orderlies rushed in to treat him, cutting open his waterproof immersion suit to find that his main injury was to his leg. A comparatively young man, he'd been sent off with little knowledge of where he was going or what danger he'd been running.

THE PARAS DIG IN

Robert Fox: Sunday 23 May

The Paras have makeshift shelters in the rocks in the hills. The ground is so soggy here the trenches fill with water if they're dug too deep. I visited one position looking across Falkland Sound, manned by a team operating Blowpipes – hand-held missiles. 'You're the first bloke we've seen for two days, mate, have a wet,' was the greeting as they brewed their tea. Despite the windswept conditions, the men are in good heart. The Brigade Commander, Brigadier Julian Thompson, told me while visiting the Paras he thought the operation had been very successful to date. For nearly two days there have been no serious Argentine attacks. Rapier anti-aircraft missiles have now been established all round the anchorage.

More details are coming to light about the first day's fighting in which the frigate HMS *Ardent* was lost. I saw survivors of her crew come abroad the *Canberra*. Two young petty officers told me how they'd been bombarding Goose Green when they were attacked by several waves of Mirage fighters. A bomb struck the stern, depriving the ship of her power, her missiles and her guns. And when the last wave of aircraft dived, the ship had only a team of five machine-gunners led by the NAAFI manager. As the Mirages pressed their attack, two were shot down by Sea Harriers. 'The boys fought like young tigers' was the verdict of an exhausted officer as he boarded the *Canberra*.

Out in the field an Argentinian surrendered to one of the parachute battalion, and I understand two more have surrendered this morning. Their unit had been heavily shelled by the navy during the landing. The army, navy and air force will clearly be strengthening local air superiority before ground forces make their next move.

THE LOSS OF *ANTELOPE*
Brian Hanrahan: Tuesday 25 May

Antelope went the way of the two other British ships lost so far, destroyed in a fire started by enemy action. She was hit on Sunday afternoon when the Argentine air force resumed its raids on San Carlos Bay; although only a few planes broke through the defensive screen, *Antelope* was badly damaged. She came slowly up the bay, making smoke, her main mast bent over at an angle. There were holes along her side and she dropped anchor half a mile away. About an hour after dark there was an explosion on board, a fire started amidships and spread swiftly from the waterline to the deck. Smoke and steam sent a grey cloud drifting over the water and through it, the searchlights of helicopters probed for survivors. Landing craft came alongside to lift off the crew and transfer them to other ships nearby. We could just see the figures crossing the deck, silhouetted by the flames. Other ships and more helicopters quartered the sea around about, in case anyone was in the cold waters. It was a courageous and

41

orderly rescue against the ever-present danger of further explosion.

After everyone had been got clear there were explosions. They sent sparks and flames high into the air and the ship burnt white-hot through the night. On the deck near me, as I imagine on others in the anchorage, small knots of men looked on in horror as the ship died. At dawn it was still glowing red, the side ripped open, everything above deck-level reduced to mangled, black metal. On Monday afternoon *Antelope* broke her back, and as the sea rushed in a white cloud erupted, the hot metal was finally cooled, the bows and the stern rose from the surface, and then slowly sank.

GOOSE GREEN AND DARWIN

A week after the landings at San Carlos, British forces broke out of the bridgehead and achieved one of the most famous victories of the war. No. 2 Para took Goose Green after bitter fighting against Argentine forces that turned out to be three times stronger in number than expected. Their Commanding Officer, Colonel 'H' Jones was killed in an inspiringly brave attack on enemy machine-gun positions.

Robert Fox was close to Colonel 'H' in the last days of his life and his reports tell much about an extraordinary man.

The BBC, not for the first time in the war, came under strong criticism for a broadcast that was said to give premature news of the attack. These were especially difficult and dangerous days for the two front-line corres-pondents. It was soon recognised that the report had not originated with them, but with sources in London. After sailing in different ships and being attached to different units, Hanrahan and Fox were now in the same locations for the first time, and each gave his own account of the scenes at Goose Green after liberation.

With the seizure of Mount Kent and other high points, the way to Port Stanley opened up. Michael Nicholson of ITN, whose reports were available to the BBC under 'pooling' arrangements, said that British forces 'could see through their binoculars Argentine troops eating lunch'. A writer to *Points of View*, perhaps seeking light relief amidst so much grim news, claimed to have heard the phrase as 'they could see Argentine troops eating lunch through their binoculars'. One of the smaller jokes of the war.

LIBERATION OF GOOSE GREEN

Robert Fox: Sunday 30 May

At one end of the Goose Green settlement a Union Jack now flies above a school; and at the other end the flag of the Second Battalion, the Parachute Regiment. After a whole day's bitter fighting and a morning's delicate surrender negotiations, the cheer of liberation came in the early afternoon. Women handed round cups of tea in Royal Wedding mugs; children carried round tins of cakes and biscuits to the young Paras, their faces still camouflaged and their eyes bleary with exhaustion.

For nearly a month, the 114 people had been shut into the community hall by the Argentines. Their houses had been raided, with furniture smashed and excrement on the floor. The store had been looted, the Argentine troops were underfed, and in one house used by pilots it seemed the officers were hoarding tinned food. The Argentines committed acts of petty meanness, smashing and stealing radios and shooting up a shepherd from a helicopter as he tended his sheep. Now the prisoners are being made to clear up the mess they made in the settlements.

The surrender came after a 14-hour battle the previous day. It began before dawn – a full battalion assault on an enemy twice as numerous as expected, almost 1500 in all and very well dug in. The attack began under naval gunfire, and shells lit the sky as the Paras moved forward. But in the daylight they were on their own, covered only by guns and mortars. The enemy were falling back slowly to prepared positions. At each post their own mortars had been ranged perfectly. Time and again we were pinned down by fire from mortars and anti-aircraft guns. I was with the battalion headquarters, and if we were within ten feet of death from shrapnel and shells once, we were there forty times.

Around mid-morning we were pinned down in a fold in the land by mortar fire when the first prisoners and casualties came in. The prisoners made a pathetic sight, looking for their own dead and preparing them for burial. This was interrupted by an air attack from Pucara aircraft. As they swung across the sky every firearm available opened up to no effect, and the two planes shot down a

Scout helicopter just beyond our ridge. In mid-afternoon we were again pinned down by mortar fire among some gorse bushes.

We were told that the commanding officer, Lt-Col. H. Jones, always known as 'H', had been shot by machine-gunners as he led an attack against machine-gun nests which had held up the battalion for over half an hour. A generous, extrovert man, he died in the manner in which he led his battalion, in peace and war. Before the operation he confided to me that, while he was eager to get on with the attack, he was worried about achieving one hundred per cent success with such a complex plan of attack. The victory is entirely his. 'It was his plan that worked,' said the Second-in-Command, Major Chris Keeble. 'He was the best, the very best,' said Staff Sergeant Collins. In the evening they brought his body down from the hillside, a soldier walking in front, his weapon pointed to the ground. The silhouette of this silent ceremony the most indelible image of the day.

The architect of the surrender was acting CO, Major Keeble. At midday we walked across the Goose Green airfield. My colleague David Norris of the *Daily Mail* and I were asked to be civilian witnesses. Within two hours the senior Argentine officer, Air Vice-Commodore Wilson Doser Pedroza, had agreed surrender terms. He paraded his airmen and gave a political speech. And after singing the national anthem, they threw their guns and helmets to the ground. There were whoops of joy from one group as they threw their weapons down. They were glad to be going home, they said. Senior British officers, watching, were amazed at the numbers, nearly three times the strength of the ground forces they had been led to expect in the area. There were two lessons for the future: first, the tenacity with which the Argentines held well-prepared defensive positions; second, there were rivalries between their services and between conscripts, officers and NCOs.

But the liberation of Goose Green was due above all to the courage of the Second Battalion of the Parachute Regiment. They carried out a type of attack not seen since the last war, and its success was due to the dash and heroism of their commander and of the men who fought and died with him.

On a wintry sunny evening, the men who died freeing Port Darwin and Goose Green were buried together in a mass grave on a bare hillside above the anchorage at San Carlos Water. The funeral lasted a few minutes. As the dead were carried to the grave by company commanders and soldiers of the Second Battalion, Parachute Regiment, there was no oration or firing party over the grave. The battalion padre, the Reverend David Cooper, read the roll of the dead from No. 2 Para, the Army Air Corps and 59 Field Squadron, Royal Engineers. First was the name of the CO, Lieutenant-Colonel H. Jones, who died assaulting a machine-gun post. Then there was the adjutant, Captain David Wood, who died alongside the colonel. Then their fellow officers and men, a helicopter pilot and a sapper. At the end, the RSM threw a handful of earth into the grave and the Marines and Paras saluted in silence. In the bay a frigate quietly trained her guns skyward against a possible air-raid. The Paras are anxious that their dead comrades should not remain in an anonymous mass-grave here at Ajax Bay. 'They must be taken back to England,' one company commander said. An RSM told me, 'The lads want the dead to go home. It's tradition. People will want to visit the graves.'

BOMB ALLEY

Brian Hanrahan: Monday 31 May
Interview with Gordon Clough on *PM*

CLOUGH: I asked Brian Hanrahan about the Argentine casualties at Goose Green. What was happening to the prisoners who'd been wounded?

HANRAHAN: Well, they're being moved away to a field hospital that's been set up on the edges of the bay here, and they'll then, once they've been treated and had the most immediate treatment they require, be moved off to the hospital ship, *Uganda*, which is moving into the area in order to pick up all casualties, both the British and Argentine.

CLOUGH: You will be aware, as we're aware here, of the Argentine allegation that *Uganda*'s been acting contrary to the laws of war, impeding the movement of combatants. What's the view in the fleet about that?

HANRAHAN: The view is that that would be . . . well, balderdash I think would be the way it would be put. *Uganda* has been moving in when necessary to pick up casualties, and moving out of the area again. It hasn't sat right outside the bay in a position where it might get hit by any air attack. There's been an immense effort to keep *Uganda* clear of any form of involvement in the hostilities. We, the pressmen, have even been refused permission to go and visit her because it was thought by visiting there it might be seen as part of the propaganda war, or that by military helicopters going to and fro for reasons unconnected with medical reasons, that might jeopardise its status. So a considerable attempt has been made to isolate *Uganda* from anything to do with the fighting. But it must come in close in order to pick up the casualties – some of these men are very seriously injured and they couldn't take a long helicopter flight going way out to sea. Apart from the fact that there is a risk that helicopters do go down in the sea when they fly a lot. We've lost several helicopters that way already. So far we've managed to rescue nearly all of them, apart from the one very ill-fated crash when something like more than twenty men were lost at night. But apart from that men have been recovered. But how you recover a seriously injured man from such cold water as we have, who can't help themselves, I can't imagine. So it must come in close to do that job.

CLOUGH: You mentioned that the Argentine prisoners were being transferred to a field hospital. We have reports that a field hospital has been hit by an Argentine bombing raid. Do you know anything about that?

HANRAHAN: Yes. I saw that a couple of days ago. And it was a dusk raid when a couple of planes came over the hillside, stayed within the bay for just a few seconds (they clearly were unwilling to come and make the long runs they had been making), and they dropped several bombs

47

around the place, and one of them went through the dressing station outside the field hospital. I don't think anybody was there and I don't believe any casualties were caused by it. However, other bombs were also dropped comparatively close to the area, and they certainly did cause casualties and one of them dropped in the middle of an ammunition dump, which went up and burnt away with explosions for several hours. We stood there and we watched it. We worried a great deal about the men who were close by and the hospital we knew was right alongside.

CLOUGH: You said that was a couple of days ago. Since then, from what we're hearing, there has been a reduction of the air attacks on San Carlos. Does that seem to you to point to a change of tactics on the part of the Argentine air force?

HANRAHAN: Well, the Argentine air force appears to have given up its attempts to run the full gauntlet of coming in here. We've been calling it 'bomb alley' because of the number of bombs and attacks that have been made on us. But at the same time it's been 'suicide alley' as far as the Argentine pilots are concerned. They've been losing sixty per cent of the planes that have come in. And in the last few days they've obviously stopped doing this. The rate of attrition was just too high to be continuously borne. However, what we have seen is a switch to more unorthodox tactics. There was this dusk raid where they sneaked over the hill, hit the hospital and came out again. They lost two out of four planes in doing that, so that wasn't very much good. There's been a high-level bombing raid last night, in which what we believe were Canberras came over at a considerable distance above and dropped bombs randomly. That hasn't done any damage either. But obviously it's a danger. And there was one exceedingly unorthodox raid when a Hercules transport plane came across over a ship, opened its back doors, which are normally used for putting stores in and out, and threw bombs out. That didn't do any damage either, but it's a measure of the determination and perhaps the desperation of the Argentine forces, that they were willing to deliver bombs by hand with a man picking them up and chucking them out the back trying to hit a ship.

CLOUGH: Can you tell me – when you were sitting there, in 'bomb alley' as you call it, under constant attack, can you try to explain to me, who has never been in this position, what it's like?

HANRAHAN: It was extraordinarily remote. The whole thing happens with such desperate speed. It's hard to believe that you're in the danger that you are in. When the planes come over the hillside they flash at enormous speed through the anchorage, which is a couple of miles long, they're going, it would see, at something in the region of 400 miles an hour, and dropping their bombs and firing their cannons as they go. The air fills with a kaleidoscope of different colours, as everybody in sight fires back at them. The noise is terrific. If you see the planes you're lucky. Normally they're through and gone and what you see are the trails of the missiles chasing after them. What seems to have happened is a foreshortening effect. Because of the missiles, because of the speed of the aircraft, everything happens in intensely short bursts, at very low level, because to go in and do it any other way would be sheer suicide for the pilots. So what happens is that you get these very intense bursts interspersed with enormously long periods in which nothing happens. But you know something might happen at any moment. Oddly enough, I've been on both a store ship and a warship in the course of this, and I've felt more worried and more vulnerable on the warship, which was foolish, than I did on the store ship, because on the store ship there's not much you can do except sit and wait. On the warship everybody's got tin helmets on, they've got flak jackets on, they are constantly reminded to keep their weapons primed and watching. And in that sort of atmosphere tension creeps up over you which is really quite unbelievable.

CLOUGH: What kind of effect did the taking of Goose Green have on the morale of the fleet, who presumably heard about it on the radio?

HANRAHAN: Well, they heard about it a bit before. They knew about it as it happened, but there seemed to be a lot of reports flying around on the radio which suggested it had happened before it had even started, so there's a certain amount of anger about what appears to be the leaking of information. But certainly in terms of the effect of that capture, there was a most dramatic effect. People feel a great deal happier, and after absorbing more than a week of quite heavy punishment, and a lot of anxiety, even though a lot has been handed back to the pilots who were coming in, it was a tremendous relief to see the land forces firmly established, and sufficiently well established, to go away and make a major victory, particularly one which was, I think, in military terms a remarkable victory. Troops against a defensive position, storming it, and taking against two to one odds against them, despite very, very heavy attack – there were mortars, there was machine-gun fire, there were ground-attack aircraft called in against them. It was the sort of victory which will live for a long time in the Second Paras.

CLOUGH: Let me ask you more about this anger that's being felt. I was referring actually to people hearing about it on ship-to-shore radio, rather than from the BBC. But if you're talking about World Service reports, what do people think has been going on? Do they think there's been leaking information from London, or what?

HANRAHAN: No, the impression left here is that somebody in London is releasing information that suggests that attacks are imminent. And that this had got to the stage where not only attacks are imminent, but what sort of attacks are imminent, and at whom they are directed. It was felt from the reports being heard on the radio that firm information was being given that Goose Green and Darwin were going to be attacked and shortly. The result of that is that the garrison was reinforced. It is presumed it was reinforced because of this either solid information or heavy speculation, whichever it is, and this could have been exceedingly serious for the forces here, and if it continues it might well jeopardise the action.

BRITAIN TAKES OVER 1400 PRISONERS

Brian Hanrahan: Tuesday 1 June

The British forces have been all but overwhelmed by the number of prisoners and have had to improvise a system for dealing with them. They're being flown back to San Carlos Bay – as and when helicopters are available. There they're brought aboard one of the landing ships at anchor – apprehensive men under the guard of sentries with submachine-guns – and then taken below to sit facing a wall with their hands on their heads while they're being 'processed'. One at a time they're brought forward to be stripped and searched, standing on a paper sack to ease the chill of the metal deck. They seemed well enough clad although some had holes in their boots, but most were young and painfully thin. One told his captors that all he'd had to eat in two days was a cup of rice.

Their possessions, apart from their clothes, are taken away and signed for. Even their bootlaces are removed. It seems harsh but the procedure is exactly as laid down by the Geneva Convention. The military police who have taken charge of the prisoners have copies available in English and Spanish. After that each man is labelled – the only labels available in quantity are brightly-coloured baggage tags from a P & O cruise. Then they're released into the hold, where they spend the night. And a cold and uncomfortable night it's going to be, sleeping on a metal deck normally used for stores, trying to avoid the damp patches on the floor. Those still ashore are sleeping in sheep tents. But this is just a temporary holding area until they can be transferred to a prison ship and removed from the fighting zone.

They'll have reason to welcome that: during the night, Argentina made a high-level bombing raid over the bay and one bomb exploded on a hillside not far from the ship where they're being kept.

NAPALM

Brian Hanrahan: Tuesday 1 June

It's been discovered that full preparations were under way to use napalm, a burning jelly that sticks to the skin, against British forces. Drop tanks, full of it, stand on the airstrip at Goose Green and Darwin, with the napalm trickling out on to the ground. leaving white corrosive areas where it leaked. Some of the drop tanks are specially designed for the job of delivering it. They carry 220 kilograms each. There are more than fifty home-made tanks, crudely manufactured, just a tube brought to a point and capable of carrying a hundred kilos.

British experts examining them gingerly said they appeared to be fused ready for use. In the centre of the village, we found a place where they'd been filled up. There were more tanks, some apparently charged and ready, with instructions for using them nearby. It came in a Spanish document marked 'Secret', five pages long, dated 1978, and headed 'Bombe Napalm'. It contained instructions for fitting and using napalm drop tanks to Pucara bombers which were based at Goose Green. Around them were the paraphernalia for mixing the stuff, thin plastic buckets and barrels. It requires aviation spirit, paraffin and a gel, so it sticks to the skin once it's alight. Once it's mixed it's unstable and should be used immediately. Some of the thirty-two tanks lying about were full. They'd been there for days, and there were houses just a few yards away.

Napalm is a horrifying weapon, but easy to use and effective. The British commanders say they fear there may be more stocks at Port Stanley, and Argentine forces may be turning to it as a desperate tactic. The islanders told me that some of the airmen who'd been at Goose Green had left just before the surrender.

AFTER THE BATTLE (1)

Brian Hanrahan: Tuesday 1 June

Four days after the battle, Goose Green is still a military camp, but a happy one. The Argentine positions have been taken over by the paratroopers, and groups of soldiers wander through the churned up lanes chatting cheerfully with the islanders. In the background there's the constant noise of helicopters carrying supplies in and prisoners out, and the chatter of gunfire as captured weapons are tested and taken over by the new defenders. Union Jacks flutter over the flagpoles and the air is full of the comforting smell of peat fires as the islanders return to their homes to dry up and clear out after the occupying forces. Sally McCleod, a housewife putting up her washing, turned to wave at a helicopter flying low overhead. 'It's rainy,' she said, 'but lovely.' She, like the others, had been ordered into the village hall on 1 May and kept there at gunpoint until the British arrived. Children and old people – no bedding, two toilets, a cut-off water supply, and for the first few days only biscuits to eat. They were threatened with guns but only one man was physically hurt. Some Argentine soldiers thought he had a radio so they tied him up with hide and kept him bound on the floor while bullets from the battle fell around.

What the islanders found when they got home seems to be squalor and mindless vandalism: locks shot off; beds slept in by men who kept their muddy boots on; drawers emptied all over the floor. There had been some looting but many items like radios were simply thrown out and smashed. All the food in the houses, which had been stocked up for many months, had been stolen. Today, though, the islanders were cheerfully putting things to rights, doing the washing, sorting through the debris. On the recreation ground, where the Argentine soldiers surrendered, their helmets and packs lie in lines where they were dropped. In the centre of the square is a huge mound of ammunition: hand grenades, anti-tank rockets, mortar bombs, and around it thousands and thousands of rounds of rifle bullets – so many that the soldiers sorting through it crunch across the casings as though they were on a shingle beach. There were hundreds of prisoners kept under cover in the sheep-rearing sheds at the end of the village. Working parties of visitors are being used to clear up the village hall and the litter that's everywhere.

The islanders greeted the paratroopers as a liberating army – cheering them in, pressing gifts upon them. One soldier told me he'd been given a bottle of vodka. Had he drunk it? 'After five days out there,' he said, indicating the snow-covered mountains, 'of course I did.' The Argentine forces' treatment of the islanders has killed any thought they might have had of leaving or compromising. Martin Ridge, a young man of twenty-three, put it most succinctly. 'Men have died to free this settlement. I owe it to them to stay here.'

AFTER THE BATTLE (2)

Robert Fox: Wednesday 2 June

Piles of ammunition, field artillery and machine-guns, the skeletons of wrecked Pucara aircraft, are still strewn across the little port of Goose Green. There is the occasional thud of landmines being detonated by parties of paras and prisoners. They have been collecting their dead from the battlefield, they've about 140 in number to date. In the late afternoon ten more Argentinians came in from the countryside, shivering with cold in their thin uniforms and shabby parka jackets.

Towards evening there was a loud explosion. Prisoners handling military shells had set off a pile. It's not clear whether the fuses were faulty, but it is more likely, say military officers on the scene, that booby traps had been laid. At least two Argentinians were killed, one died later in hospital, and more prisoners were severely injured. The prisoners have protested about not being moved, they are cold and suffering from lung and stomach complaints, and they are worried about the danger from Argentinian counter-attack. A delegation of four Argentinian officers have complained about their treatment, quoting the Geneva Convention, though ironically I understand that Argentina is only a partial signatory to it. The prisoners have left behind their quantities of ammunition and heavy weaponry, though most is in poor condition. Settlers say morale was not good in the Argentinian forces, with their officers often kicking and punching their men and jabbing them with bayonets.

The men of 2 Para have been relaxing for a couple of days after their assault of the enemies' fixed position. In the settlers' houses they have had the luxury of a bath and a shave. The scale of their victory is only now being appreciated. With little cover from guns and aircraft, they assaulted positions of the Argentinians – their main strategic reserve in the Falklands outside Port Stanley itself, a force of some 1600 men – but now the Paras are impatient to move on to Port Stanley itself. 'It's time to move on,' said RSM Simpson to me. 'We've had our rest and now we need to attack Stanley as soon as possible.'

WORLD TONIGHT INTERVIEW ON GOOSE GREEN

Robert Fox: Wednesday 2 June

FOX: Going into Goose Green was an act of almost foolish heroism because nobody knew quite what the strength of the opposition was. I was at the O Group, that is the Order Group, given by Colonel H. Jones the evening before, and we talked about it almost as if it were an exercise. We knew that we were going in with equal strength. The Paras knew that they would have a cover from naval gunfire and we had three artillery pieces of our own. We expected to meet about five or six thousand men at the maximum. And then we all went to sleep in a little house called Camilla Creek House down the road. I actually slept next to H. Jones. It was one of those ludicrous, almost schoolboy, episodes. We woke up in the middle of the night and we heard lots of jokes about what we would do when we got there and what kind of clothes we were going to wear in the morning. H. Jones confided to me: 'Well, this is the only time I've ever done something like this.' I said that I

55

was a bit worried because I'd never been in a battle before, and he said, 'I'm worried too, mate, because I've got to get in there and lead these men and get them through it. I have every confidence in my men, but it's such a difficult plan of battle.'

Then, at two o'clock in the morning, we went down the path and we first knew that we were in battle when the illuminating shells came in overhead from the frigate, and then it was absolutely like Guy Fawke's Day because the Argentinians from their fixed positions put up one flare after another. The thing that had happened was that they had forewarning, they'd got themselves dug in and they fought well from six positions. When the plan of battle changed, they weren't so good. They had very good artillery and, as we went along the foreshore, went up the heath to the green, to Goose Green, we were observed by at least two or three observation posts in the mountains opposite over the bay. So when four or five of us put our heads up, there was a ping and a crunch and a whizz, because you could hear the wretched stuff flying through the air, sometimes only eighteen inches above one's head. They were seeing you every single time, and it's a mercy that not more of us were killed. At one time I was just swimming through gorse bushes but there was nothing we could do to get away with it. I've made a friend for life though with the RSM, RSM Simpson. We've hugged each other and fallen into trenches together so often now that we can't part from this anything but soul mates.

GORDON CLOUGH: I gather that, as the battle went on, Bob, there was one particular Argentine gun nest that was proving very obstinate?

FOX: Well, it wasn't one nest. It was a ring of six positions just above Port Darwin. What happened was that two companies were in the plain below them, and Colonel H. Jones, in his flamboyant manner, decided that this was the time to go and pick out these machine-gun positions, otherwise his men would be wiped out by mortar and artillery, and he felt he couldn't ask people to do something that he wouldn't do himself. So he turned himself into a platoon commander, went with his adjutant and assaulted a machine-gun position and, alas, was killed.

CLOUGH: We've read quite a lot, Bob, in the newspaper reports about the bravery, not to say heroism, of the young men who volunteered to go with him.

FOX: Yes. Well, there is a very sad story there. It wasn't exactly in that attack, but it was at the same time as this particular attack that H was doing. It was young Lieutenant Barry. Two Argentinians hoisted a flag and we understand that he put down his weapon and went forward with an NCO to take the surrender and somebody got up behind the two Argentinians and opened fire, jumped up on to the lip of the trench, fired at the whole patrol and then jumped back again.

CLOUGH: Take me now to the surrender, Bob, if you would, to the formal ceremony of surrender.

FOX: The formal ceremony of surrender was a most peculiar occasion. It's one of the things, I suppose, that I will never forget in my life, probably that and the image of Colonel Jones's body being brought down. I was asked by Major Keeble from the beginning to go up there because he was worried about the language, and I don't speak terrific Spanish but my Italian, in fact, carried me through and I was one of the two on the British side that could follow the whole thing. And so he wanted me to watch that and he wanted to make sure that the military weren't going to be accused of malfaisance or wrongdoing, so I said, Yes, willingly I'd come along.

When we got to the airfield, what they really wanted was very strange. The thing that we wanted above all was the safe passage of the civilian people. If we were going to have to fight our way into Goose Green, we did not want to fight with civilians there. And that was the first thing. And what they were most worried about was having the due ceremony for their surrender so that they could call their men to parade, they could call them to attention, they could harangue them with political speeches, they could sing the Argentinian National Anthem, they could shout 'Viva' for Argentina, and then throw down their arms. And this is, in fact, what they got.

It was this ceremony, with this element of self-respect, which was the most important aspect of the surrender. One of the officers confided to us that they felt that they had been sold out, sold out completely by the regime in Argentina, and, of course, as we saw from the physical actions, the joy with which some of these young men threw down their belts and weapons and their helmets, that they were very, very glad to get out of it indeed. They did not surrender reluctantly, many of these people.

CLOUGH: Well, apart from being a fighting army winning battles, you're also in a very real sense a liberating army. What did you see of the freeing of the Goose Green settlers?

FOX: When the surrender was taken, things were very formal. Then suddenly it became terribly relaxed and informal. We agreed that the prisoners should go back and have their food and pack up their belongings, and while they were doing that the first company of the Paras came in and it was a wonderful sight to see. They looked very disciplined and they looked very cool and in control and they took up a defensive position. They were crouching on one knee. Then the women came out with cups of tea and the children came out with tins of sweets, enormous sweets, handing around to these young men, bleary-eyed, some of them injured, biscuits and so on, and the tea was literally flowing, in the special Falkland Island Royal Wedding Mugs, stamped Falkland Islands on the back. And they put a little flag up on the school, and I met a lot of people at that time and they told me of their joy and their disbelief that they'd got through it. They had, indeed, got through it without having any serious injury or anyone being killed.

CLOUGH: But they got through it at great personal discomfort and, I should think, probably fear, these 114 people locked up in the hall for nearly four weeks. What did they tell you about that time?

FOX: I've talked to a lot of people about this. They were

locked up in the Community Hall after the first Harrier attack, after the first month of occupation. The Harriers really do terrify the Argentinians, there's no doubt about that. They weren't particularly mean at first, although it was very much you do as we say. You eat when we say, you can go out and exercise when we say. One of the worst cases happened on the day of the battle itself when a shepherd was taken from his house. He'd been allowed back to get some belongings and rather rashly he started listening to the BBC to hear what, in fact, was going on. Some young soldiers rushed in, accused him of signalling to the fleet and kicked him rather brutally, and then tied him up with a halter, his legs tied to his wrists, so he couldn't move, and every time things went badly in the battle they jabbed him with their boots and shoved a gun into his back, and it was only after the battle was over that they released his legs and gave him a meal, some gruel.

CLOUGH: Let me end by asking you, in a way, a personal question, but not personal to you only but personally to all of them, all the men who are fighting. It's the old daft questions. How has it felt? I mean, have you felt frightened? Have you felt exhilarated?

FOX: There was a marvellous thing when we were by the gorse bushes. And it was the third time that we were shelled intensively. That's when I had the odd three-footer and five-footer – by that I mean something coming in within three or five foot of me. Now a young marine sapper handed me a bit of shrapnel. He said, 'That one's yours, mate. It missed you by eighteen inches.' And I said, 'Thank you very much.' I don't have it, needless to say, because I'd rather forget about such things. Now his mate came out of the gorse bushes and said, 'I've learnt a helluva lot about myself which I didn't realise in the last ten minutes.' But this sapper, he was the original British Tom. He was cleaning his gun; he had his back to the gorse bushes. We were being shelled and mortared and he was putting himself on a brew, and he said to me and my colleague from the *Daily Mail*, David Norris, who was down behind me, he said, 'Are you frightened, mate?' We said, 'Well, we're not frightened, if you're not frightened.

You tell us you're not frightened.' And this banter went on for ten minutes and it was a strange game of chicken. And we played this game and he said, 'Well, I think I am frightened, because I think they're getting too close. They've kept up this . . . this kind of pantomime for too long.'

The fact is that that kind of fire, it's not like something that takes you by surprise. Once you have started it's like swimming. But it concentrates the mind wonderfully and you really cannot bother. I mean, you're frightened that perhaps the next one will get you and you listen to the dreadful whizz of these mortar bombs because you can hear the mortar bomb that's coming in to you and you just have to pray and say, 'Well, if it's got my name written on it.' It sounds corny, terrible old clichés, but it's absolutely true that there is nothing you can do. There is no way you can move because if it's going to get you, it'll get you.

CLOUGH: Bob, you haven't been in the forces, I think. What do you think of them now?

FOX: It's very strange. They regard me as something of an oddity and I think that's probably quite right. The thing is it's very easy to slip into their way of thinking in many respects. In other respects it can help because you are not an officer, you're not a serving man, you're somebody to talk to, you're somebody to swear at if necessary. It's somebody to let off steam with. Now, the odd sort of thing that I've found about the Paras, and they've had a fearsome reputation I know, but amongst the officers and many of the men I have found some of the most civilised men that I've ever been in a tight corner with in my life. The standard of personal generosity, of kindness, of respect, strange to say, of respect for human life, is of a very high degree indeed, and I think that says a lot for their efficiency. That is why they are such good fighting troops, because they're fighting troops who care about each other desperately as individuals.

VISIT TO A FIELD HOSPITAL
Brian Hanrahan: Thursday 3 June
Shown on TV News 19 June

The field hospital had been set up in an abandoned refrigeration plant and the wounded rushed to it by helicopter. Some from Goose Green, some from more forward positions. In ten days more then 200 men had been treated there. We arrived in time to see the hundredth major operation.

SURGEON: As these high-velocity missiles go through limbs they create a lot of dead muscle which has to be removed, because otherwise it just festers and goes gangrenous and can cause an awful lot of problems. There's another Argentinian casualty with what looks like a shrapnel wound in the leg. I think he's basically very lucky.

HANRAHAN: Lucky?

SURGEON: Yes, because from what we've seen of the Argentine medical facilities the treatment that some of the enemy casualties have had has been inadequate to say the least. Instead of removing dead muscle they've simply closed wounds with metal clips, and this is a recipe for disaster as any surgeon will tell you. The senior surgeon here is Lt Bill McGregor who is very experienced from the Middle East and Northern Ireland and has really done a magnificent job in looking after the younger surgeons, for some of whom this is the first experience of battle surgery. And as you can see, the conditions are somewhat arduous. The light is limited, we've only got a small 6-kilowatt generator outside and fuel for that is in short supply, and the floors are not of the standard that you would expect to see even in the grounds of a hospital back home. They're very grubby. But we're dealing with fit young men who've got good resistance to infection and they simply need this surgery to help them survive later.

HANRAHAN: Surgeon Commander Rick Jolly, who showed us round, had a proud boast. Everybody who'd reached this hospital alive had left alive.

JOLLY: We set up here and began operating the the first day after the landing, and things were quiet at first and then on the third day we were attacked, as you know, and we had by then completed around twenty operations under general anaesthesia, as well as a lot of minor injured.

In addition we had taken the casualties from *Antelope* and from *Coventry*. When the building was attacked we then had to deal with casualties from this attack, and during the course of a long hard night's operating we were told that there was first one bomb and then a second bomb two wards away from where you're standing now.

HANRAHAN: Can you give me some idea how many operations you were doing per hour?

JOLLY: No, we just worked as long as there was business waiting outside, and the grand total, which has been passed this morning, of 100 operations under general anaesthetic.

HANRAHAN: Major operations?

JOLLY: Yes. And some surgery of the highest calibre under conditions that I can only describe as appalling. I think the President of the Royal College of Surgeons would be very proud to see men who hold the degree of his college working the way they worked here. Flexibility, sense of humour and tremendous determination.

HANRAHAN: It's a question I have to ask you – priority was also given to British wounded first?

JOLLY: Well, yes. During the day we were constantly subjected to air attack and we felt that the Argentine wounded could wait until nightfall when conditions were considerably easier. Those that had to be operated on straightaway were operated on and the surgeons did their cutting wearing tin hats. And every time an air-raid alert sounded non-essential staff went out and patients on trestles were lowered to the floor, but the surgeons carried on cutting.

HANRAHAN: How many have you lost here, that came in wounded?

JOLLY: I'm proud to say that everyone who has made it here alive has made it out alive, despite some wounds and injuries which were horrific.

HANRAHAN: (to Argentine MO) Are you happy, you are a medical officer?

ARGENTINE MO: Yes.

HANRAHAN: And are you happy with what you see, treatment is good? Are you happy with the treatment?

ARGENTINE: Doctors are better.

HANRAHAN: The doctors are better? But you're happy. English doctors look after you well? And the medical assistants?

ARGENTINE: Yes.

HANRAHAN: Around the edges of the buildings, men on makeshift beds waited until they were fit to move on to the hospital ship, *Uganda*. The space here was needed. There cannot be continued fighting without many more dead and wounded.

And more fighting it seems there must be. *Canberra* has returned to San Carlos Water to disembark another 2000 troops, a part of the Fifth Infantry Brigade. The Guards, who had begun their voyage from England in the *QE2*, finished it in landing craft, moving across the misty bay to advance forward, taking over from the troops already holding the ground. All day there was a steady march of men, fresh men ready for combat. This new landing, every bit as great as the first wave, doubled the number of troops ashore. Their arrival gave the British command a chance to regroup and, for the first time, outnumber the Argentine defenders.

By now so many troops and supplies had come ashore that the beach and the tracks were a morass of mud, evidence of the weight of the British advance. But there's no intention of getting stuck in First World War trench warfare. The Gurkhas are already here digging in across the island. Some of their forward positions are within sight of Port Stanley. The advance continues.

THE MARCH ON STANLEY

Robert Fox: *World Tonight* Saturday 5 June

FOX: Think of any moorland in England, Wales, Scotland or Ireland, think of it under permanent mist, drizzle, rain, think of the boggiest part of that moorland, and you've just about got the predominant terrain of East Falkland where these troops have been marching. They marched through this grey mud, and men with the toughest feet find that they've got blisters at the end of it. Commanding officers of commandos and battalions are now instructing their men to take the minimum with them on their battle order. But they are taking a great deal of ammunition, they take their personal weapons, and it really is a very considerable achievement to march dozens of kilometres a day. This is the one thing that has really caught out the Argentinians and a thing that they have proved themselves incapable of doing. Coming out from Stanley to places like Goose Green they commandeered local vehicles, particularly Land Rovers, and got even those bogged down. The British, for the most part, although they've used a great number of helicopters, have relied on Shanks' pony. And they've stood up to this kind of march very, very well. They are the cream of our assault troops – the commandos and the paratroopers – they have been prepared for this, but it is quite an ordeal, because it is this continuous Irish mist and drizzle and rain, as well as the oozing mud. There is no part of the Falklands, I personally believe, having been ashore for a fortnight, that is dry at all.

GORDON CLOUGH: Up there on the heights of Mount Kent, Fox dug in with the Paras and saw for himself the enormously impressive resources which are poised to sweep down on Port Stanley.

FOX: There is a tremendous artillery preparation and it is very dramatic to see, coming over this moorland, the helicopters with the guns slung under them, and then with rope slings underneath them, carrying thousands and thousands of rounds of ammunition. When you're actually in a battle, and I followed 2 Paras to Goose Green during the battle there, you don't see your guns. But you get to know how to listen to them, you do literally hear artillery shells and frequently mortars whistling overhead. You get to know what an explosion of a gun discharging is, and then what the explosion of a shell landing is. This is one slight disadvantage for artillery from this peculiar climate and terrain of the Falklands, in that the peat bog is such that it does muffle some of the effect of the ground-landing shells, as both sides have discovered. But the kind of barrage which is now being prepared for Port Stanley is quite formidable. One of the COs of the commando units thinks that it is probably bigger than any we employed in Korea, and measures up to World War Two standards.

CLOUGH: Is it then a scene of almost continuous activity at the spearhead position?

FOX: The pace if anything is increasing. The logistic arrangement has been a miracle, getting this size of force ashore with the resources available so far from home.

CLOUGH: Have you managed to see Stanley yourself, either directly or through binoculars?

FOX: No. You are getting now very much dependent on the weather for that. From Mount Kent they can see Port Stanley when the mist clears. The mist is rather with us at this time of year. I gather you've been having tremendous heat waves. It made us very jealous here because we were facing the first of our snows. I can assure you that the thing that worries me most after the battle of Goose Green was not a renewal of hostilities. We thought as we camped with 2 Para overnight then there was a serious possibility of frostbite, of hypothermia, exposure, because these are the real problems that every force out in the open is facing. British Forces are very well provided with clothing, special Arctic clothing, sleeping bags and so forth. From the evidence that I have seen the Argentinians are for the most part in a pathetic plight. They have sort of plastic children's sleeping bags if they're well off, provided obviously by the individual families themselves. They have rather inferior parkas based on the US Army model, but they seem desperately thin. They seem very damp and very cold. And whatever else is going on in Port Stanley at the moment, the commanders really must be worried about the continuing effect of bad weather, of hunger and of course disease.

THE GURKHAS

Brian Hanrahan: Monday 7 June

The Gurkhas have been given the task of protecting the British rear. From their base they fly out daily in army Scout helicopters on search and destroy missions looking for groups of Argentine soldiers who were outflanked in the main advance. They're not worrying about twos or threes, but only formations big enough to be a threat. I watched one group preparing for their airborne patrol being briefed in Gurkhali by one of their officers. As he talked softly to them, one produced his kukri and slit open a tube of camouflage cream which they passed around, smearing it on their faces and exchanging banter. Then they mounted their helicopters and left, setting down from time to time to check a cottage or an abandoned tent. But this patrol, like the others for the past few days, failed to discover anything except abandoned arms and ammunition.

Privately, the British officers doubt that the men in the hills are likely to do anything except surrender. They say the Argentine soldiers who gave up at Goose Green seemed happier in captivity than they were in their own army. According to them, the ordinary Argentine conscript was left very much to fend for himself while the officers and the NCOs did all right. Among the profession- al soldiers of the British army there's amazement that no cleaning kit for their weapons was found on the 1400 Argentine prisoners, something borne out by the state of their guns. Many are so rusty that they're unusable. One soldier who spent two hours cleaning up a captured rifle said that when he began he couldn't move a single part, not even the safety catch.

The feeling among the British officers is that the lack of motivation among the Argentine soldiers explains their failure to do anything to check the rapid British advance. They say that if the defending forces were pushed forwards to face the British troops the evidence suggests that they would surrender once they're away from their comman- der's influence.

BLUFF COVE

As the British forces prepared for the final attack on Port Stanley, Brian Hanrahan reported the daring capture of Bluff Cove, an important military objective. Hardly had he got through with a delayed dispatch when the horrifying news broke of the Argentine air attack on the two landing ships, *Sir Galahad* and *Sir Tristram*. Fifty British lives were lost, mainly Welsh Guardsmen.

Brain Hanrahan's TV team were near enough for cameraman Bernard Hesketh to catch the Argentine planes swooping in and the unforgettable scenes of rescue by helicopter and boat. Robert Fox, on board HMS *Fearless*, saw survivors who said they had not even time to put on their anti-flash masks.

The shock and the surprise were all the greater as there had been a lull in the Argentine air attacks, and these were the first troopships to be hit, despite all the horrors of 'bomb alley'. It still took only one more week for the surrender of Port Stanley . . .

CAPTURE OF BLUFF COVE

Brian Hanrahan: Sunday 6 June

The capture of Bluff Cove was brought about by good luck, great daring and military opportunism. It's a tiny settlement, but it controls the last bridge on the road to Port Stanley and, after the capture of Goose Green, the next major objective of the British forces. From Goose Green it was thirty-five miles away, a long haul across open country in clear view of Argentine observation posts which could pull down air and artillery strikes. But the British Brigadier, Tony Wilson, discovered that Bluff Cove was undefended and noticed the clouds had blanked out the view of the observation posts in the mountains. Thinking that only a fool fights for territory he can get for free, he gambled on getting his men there before an Argentine garrison moved in.

There were only a few hours of daylight left and almost no helicopters to carry his men forward. But as luck would have it, a big Chinook arrived to take away prisoners. The Brigadier hijacked it, crowded his men aboard, far more than it was ever meant to carry, and shoved spare mortar bombs and ammunition into their arms. Then, with more men crammed into tiny Scout helicopters, the force, which numbered about a hundred, raced for Bluff Cove with orders to get in and hang on. They arrived just before dusk and waited tensely through the night for a counter-attack from the main Argentine garrison, numbered in thousands and just a dozen miles up the road. But the counter-attack never came. And next morning more men were sent up but told to do nothing to draw attention to themselves. Let the Argentinians think it was just a patrol were the orders.

So far, the vital bottleneck on the road to Stanley had been taken without a shot being fired. The gamble had paid off. The problem was how to build up this toehold into a secure position. The bulk of the Fifth Infantry Brigade was still behind the mountains in San Carlos Bay – 3000 men, all their stores and ammunition had to be moved right across the island. The answer was to put them on ships and sail them round to land within range of the guns of Port Stanley. It was such a hazardous operation that the ships themselves had to stand off by Lively Island

and send landing craft across the channel by night. It should have been a four-hour trip but a storm blew up. High seas, heavy rain and driving wind. It stretched the journey out to six hours, and to some veterans it was the worst in their memory. At one point the flotilla of landing craft came under mortar artillery fire and had to scatter, but they all got there safely, if a little seasick and shaken.

Even more remarkably, another battalion repeated the journey the following night. The operation saved days, if not weeks, of cross-country marches and airlifts. The risks had been great, but the reward was enormous. A full brigade of fresh troops installed on the doorstep of the enemy with all its support.

THE ATTACK ON THE LANDING CRAFT

Robert Fox: Wednesday 9 June

It was the fiercest Argentinian air offensive for more than a week and one of the heaviest of the campaign. Up to seventeen Mirages and Skyhawk A4s were launched from the Argentinian mainland during the day. In late afternoon Skyhawks struck at two landing support ships, *Sir Galahad* and *Sir Tristram*, as they were unloading at Fitzroy Settlement. Survivors say there was less than thirty seconds warning before bombs hit the accommodation quarters – one landing on the main cargo deck of *Sir Galahad*. Smoke and flames choked the corridors within minutes, as helicopters and boats strove to get the injured and survivors to the shore where they were tended in field dressing stations.

Soon both *Sir Galahad* and *Sir Tristram*, her sister ship – at the time largely empty of stores – were alight. The worst casualties were being shipped by helicopter to the hospital at San Carlos. I saw survivors as they came aboard HMS *Fearless*. They said there was not even time to put on their anti-flash masks. They said that the attacking Skyhawks had appeared to pull up – to toss their bombs at the ships, rather than aim them directly. They praised the work of the helicopter pilots returning again and again through the heavy smoke to pick up the injured. And the doctors and medical assistants who worked into the dark at the first-aid posts.

During the day a landing craft from HMS *Fearless*, plying along the coast, was sunk by a missile from a Mirage, and a number of the crew are missing. The number of missing, injured and dead from the raids is still to be announced.

In one of the first raids of the day, Mirages were seen to attack the frigate, HMS *Plymouth*. Several bombs dropped and her funnel was hit by a shell which sent clouds of smoke and steam skywards, as she came into the San Carlos anchorage here. Fires were controlled and all weapon systems – Sea Cat missiles and the 4.5-inch guns – were working. One crewman was reported badly injured, several slightly. In the fight one Mirage was downed by her Sea Cat missiles. Six more were seen to be destroyed in the fighting throughout the day. Harriers struck three in one flight and the fourth hit the sea as the pilot seemed to look back for his colleagues. Four more Argentinian planes were hit and possibly brought down before they reached the Argentinian coast.

The timing of the air-raid has been a surprise. It's surprising, too, that such a disproportionate amount of the fighting on the Argentinian side is being done by their air force, and at considerable cost. It is hard to see how long such an air force can go on accepting losses of between forty and sixty per cent of the total number of planes sent out on a day's missions.

HEROIC RESCUERS

Brian Hanrahan: Wednesday 9 June
Shown on TV News 24 June

Skyhawks, four or five, came low across the bay to bomb the two landing ships unloading men and supplies. Although missiles were fired, proper air defences hadn't yet been installed. One of the ships, *Sir Galahad*, burst into flames immediately. The ship had been carrying two companies of the Welsh Guards. Although she was anchored for several hours they were still aboard. The helicopters, which had been moving equipment forward, now flocked to help rescue survivors. Black smoke poured out as the Guards' ammunition started to ignite. Despite the risk, the helicopters disappeared into the black cloud trying to pull men from the waters. Again and again the pilots risked their lives to save others.

On the cliff tops medical staff waited for the helicopters to bring the casualties to them. In the middle of the airlift another air-raid was called, but the orderlies kept working, ignoring the crates of ammunition stacked in the grass around about. Many of the injuries were burns. So sudden was the attack there'd not been time for the crew to put on their anti-flash masks. Around in the water orange liferafts started to drift back to the ship. The helicopters used their rotors to fan the light rubber boats back out of harm's way towards the shore. Once the casualties were clear, the helicopters brought in other survivors, among them the bewildered members of the Chinese crew. Like many of the Fleet Auxiliaries, *Sir Galahad* recruited from Hong Kong. In the confusion it took hours to find out who had survived and who had not. The priority was to save the living, not count the dead.

The fire, fanned by the wind, spread at tremendous speed along the ship. If the shore hadn't been so close, the loss of life could have been even worse. Throughout the whole rescue there was the constant crack of ammunition and the sound of bigger explosions aboard *Sir Galahad*. It took several hours to gather up all the boats and pull them into the shore. The medics waded out into the cold water checking if anyone was hurt. Fortunately there was only one man badly hurt among them. After treatment on the beach he was taken away strapped to an armoured car which climbed away up the hillside. The rest were shaken, some hysterical – they'd had to listen to their colleagues trapped below.

But that wasn't the end of it. The other landing ship, *Sir Tristram*, began to smoke. It had been hit in the same raid, although the fire took longer to gain a hold. But that ship, too, was lost burning fiercely in the night. In a week of raids at San Carlos, not a single store ship or troopship had been sunk. Now, two had been lost in a single raid.

TRAWLER IN SERVICE
Brian Hanrahan: Wednesday 9 June

We sailed up to the forward positions on an elderly island trawler, the *Monsoonon*. Normally she carried wool, sheep and stores around the islands, but in the last week she has been pressed into service first by Argentina and then by Britain. When the Argentinians abandoned her she was immobilised with a rope around her propeller but divers, with the help of a young girl from one of the settlements, took it in turns to go down in their wet suits and hack it off.

With a company of Gurkhas crowded into the hold, sitting on their packs on the drums of fuel and even on Land Rovers (the tracks are too bad for speedy driving), we set off for Fitzroy across the vital bridge from Bluff Cove. For the Gurkhas, who had already marched for two days to reach the ship, it was a useful lift, but whether they appreciated it was more doubtful – they're dreadful sailors. But as soon as they got aboard they slept, stretched out across the foothills of packs on the floor of the hold. It was an uneventful journey, with the flag of the Fifth Infantry flying in the sunset as the Task Force's most improbable ship went to war, part of the private navy of the Fifth Infantry Brigade.

But the next day the Argentine air force, which had been quiet for nearly ten days, returned to the attack with a series of air-raids around the islands. The British counted seven planes down, they thought another four had been damaged; but they took losses themselves. Three ships were hit and damaged, two of them landing ships unloading troops.

SURRENDER OF PORT STANLEY

Hanrahan and Fox had still to return to ships offshore to file their dispatches. After two and a half days marching with the Paras, Robert Fox broke off to report the long walk that took the Argentine defenders of Port Stanley completely by surprise. The two correspondents saw the final battle from different vantage points on the high ground above Port Stanley. They reported the sudden final collapse of Argentine resistance and were in Port Stanley for the triumphal entry of the tired, foot-slogging British forces. It was Fox who suggested in his radio interview with the Force Commander, Major-General Jeremy Moore, that it had been 'a damn close-run thing'. The General remembered Wellington's phrase when he came to talk to Brian Hanrahan for TV.

In the next few days both reported on the reactions of the relieved and grateful Falklanders; the plight of the thousands of Argentine prisoners soon to be shipped home on board the *Canberra*; and the minefields and other signs of the unwelcome presence of the the Argentine invaders . . .

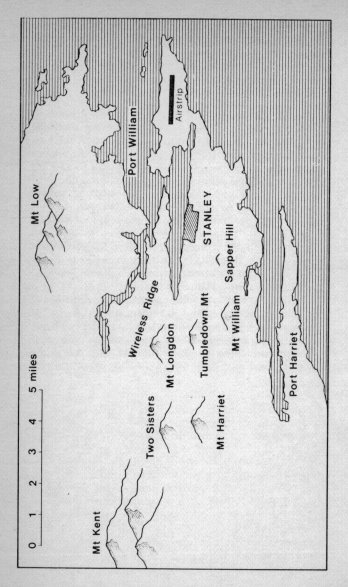

THE FINAL BATTLE

Brian Hanrahan: Monday 14 June

The commander of the British land forces, Major-General Jeremy Moore, made a hazardous night-time flight through a snowstorm to negotiate the surrender at Port Stanley. Afterwards, he sent this message to London, and to the Naval Task Force commanders:

'In Port Stanley at nine pm Falkland time, tonight, the 14th June, that's about one o'clock in London, Major-General Menendez surrendered to me all Argentine armed forces in East and West Falklands together with their impedimenta. Arrangements are in hand to assemble the men for return to Argentina, to gather their arms and equipment, and to mark and make safe their ammunitions. The Falkland Islands are once more under the government desired by their inhabitants. God save the Queen.'

The negotiations which led to this document were brief and formal. The British commander, Major-General Moore, wanted the unconditional surrender of all Argentine forces. And the Argentine garrison commander had little option but to grant it. After three days of heavy fighting, the British forces had pushed through to the outskirts of Port Stanley, and commanded all the high lands round about. From this position of strength they were able to insist that all Argentinian troops should surrender wherever they were on the islands, not just those in Port Stanley. Arrangements will begin immediately to count the Argentine prisoners and return them home.

The battle which seemed to tip the balance was the battle for Mount Tumbledown. And yesterday morning from an overlooking hill, I watched the two armies engaged in the darkness. The British advancing down the valley from my right, the Argentines dug in on the slopes of the mountain to my left. It was a battle of light and sound. First the thunder of artillery, throwing shell after shell, hundreds – no thousands, whistling down the valley to explode with a dull crunch among the Argentine defences. After several hours of bombardment, with each shell sending up a burst of flame on the mountain, the ground forces moved in. The rattle of heavy machine-guns, the explosions of the mortars, occasional pauses, and men shouting somewhere down in the darkness. But there were few pauses. The circle of fire marking the British advance moved steadily up the mountain, tightening on the defenders.

Red tracers from the surrounding hills curved towards Tumbledown, always moving ahead of the line of shells. Occasionally flares burst over the valley floor, but they showed nothing, not even a flicker of movement. In the distance I could hear the more regular thud of naval guns adding their weight to the bombardment. The ships alone fired 900 shells that night. From my position there appeared to be only one point of resistance, a machine-gun post on top of the hill; although shell after shell smacked down near it, the red tracer continued to spit out at the attackers. Through the night the battle went on, but by the morning the mountain top had been cleared, although the fighting spread along the ridge behind it. In the light I could see the shells still coming down, sending black smoke and earth, showers of it, up from the mountain. Behind, in Port Stanley itself, the smoke of fires drifted upwards. And then, quite suddenly, the resistance ceased. The Argentinians were retreating not only from Tumbledown, but from the next objective, Mount William, and also from Sapper Hill, the last high ground almost on the outskirts of Stanley itself.

The artillery moved their target to follow the fleeing soldiers. More British battalions were told to move in and take the rest of the ground. The paratroopers were already on the edges of the town. But just as the final stage of the advance was under way, there was a sudden flurry of signals. An air strike by the Harriers was cancelled. The big guns for the artillery fell silent for the first time in days. The advancing troops were to fire only in self-defence. They encountered no opposition. The Argentine positions were empty. And then just before four o'clock Greenwich time, that's five in London, an officer emerged from the radio tent to announce, 'Gentlemen, a white flag has been seen flying over Stanley.'

A sudden hushed pause was followed by a tremendous cheer. Ten weeks to the day after leaving Portsmouth, the British forces had recaptured Port Stanley. All that was needed now was the formal surrender, and that came within hours.

END OF THE FIGHTING

Robert Fox: Tuesday, 15 June

British troops have now moved into Stanley to disarm the thousands of Argentinian prisoners who are now being sent to the airfield, desolated with bomb craters and wrecked aircraft, two miles east of the town. This operation began almost exactly twenty-four hours after the first signs of the Argentinian collapse in the fighting on the high grounds to the west of the port.

Scots Guards, Gurkha and Paratroop units were fighting to secure Tumbledown and Mount William, well after first light. I had been watching from a promontory overlooking both peaks. The crack of small arms fire, artillery and mortar-barrage had been incessant. Suddenly the unit I was with, 45 Commando Royal Marines, was told to move in hot pursuit at thirty minutes notice. The Gurkhas had seen Argentinians fleeing back from their objective in regimental strength. The commandos set off with a column of snow vehicles through the peat bogs up the track to Stanley. The radio reported the Paras were walking on to the Stanley racecourse unopposed, that white flags had appeared over the port. Then the order, 'Secure and make safe all weapons', was given and the Royal Marines knew it was all over. On the Common one marine lifted a Union Jack. As the snow drove in, three assault engineers plotted a careful course through the minefields.

Towards evening we saw Stanley, fires burning from several parts of the town, soldiers standing at the west end prevented from going into the town by the terms of the ceasefire. Out in the streets, the Argentinians stood round quietly. Some set light to a store on the wharf and watched while small arms ammunition exploded. Several of us ran down the street to try to rouse other Argentinians sleeping there to get away and remove more ammunition. Discipline has been breaking down between Argentinian officers and men. One eyewitness, Alison King, saw conscripts turn on their officers and machine-gun houses in the east of the town.

Some seventy houses have been systematically looted. Throughout the night Argentinian military police patrolled, driving vehicles on the right, while the newly-freed settlers insisted on driving on the left. At daylight the Argentinians began streaming out to the airfield in snow and sleet to throw down their arms.

ENTRY INTO PORT STANLEY

Brian Hanrahan: Tuesday 15 June
Shown on TV News 25 June

Tuesday 15 June Stanley woke up to find it was back under British rule. The British soldiers didn't look like men who had just walked across the island but they had, every step of the way on their own two feet. Fifty miles they'd come over mountains and bogs in weather that chilled the bone and soaked the skin, and at the end of it they'd fought bravely and well.

Now they were coming in from the cold for a hot meal, a bath and a change of clothes, the first in three weeks. Everything had hinged on the fitness and resource of the marines and the paratroopers who had come ashore on that first day and never stopped walking. In the last hours before the surrender, Argentine officers and men were reported to be firing at each other. Now they were marched out to Stanley airfield in thousands. The British counted just over 6000. The Argentine officers said there were twice as many. Nobody was totally sure how many men there were, or which units they'd come from.

The airfield, out on a headland, is a desolate, wind-swept place, made worse by the wreckage of the British bombing and shelling. Stanley itself had suffered little physical damage, although the streets were filled with the evidence of the occupation. The Argentine armoured cars were left but other vehicles swiftly pressed into service by the British or the islanders.

The garrison had used the town with its civilian population to protect some of their field guns. A battery had been set up on flat ground behind houses. To begin with, the British worried little about the prisoners – disarmed and harmless they were allowed to move about. But the policy backfired. On Wednesday morning a group vandalised the

ENTRY INTO PORT STANLEY

Post Office. They broke in during the night, scattered letters, files, books and papers on the floor. They were smeared with excrement. It was pointless: most of the letters had been their own forces' mail.

The men who have been in the van of this army throughout the campaign are the Second Paras. They were the first – again – into Port Stanley, and the first to march through the streets to hold a Thanksgiving Service in the island's tiny Cathedral.

INTERVIEW WITH GENERAL MOORE

Brian Hanrahan: Tuesday 15 June
Shown on TV News 25 June

HANRAHAN: General, were you surprised at the speed – three weeks or so from start to finish – it took you to reach Stanley?

MOORE: No. I don't think I was surprised. Clearly the enemy was surprised. He was surprised because quite clearly he hadn't expected us to land that far away, and therefore had not really defended the area. I think that the reason it could be done was because he simply didn't understand that our troops would be able to do that.

HANRAHAN: You came across a way which presumably nobody expected you would be able to take?

MOORE: Yes. Clearly he didn't expect us to come across that way. Clearly he didn't expect, and one of my officers who speaks extremely good Spanish has been talking to a number of them and they believe that we came across because we had enormous numbers of helicopters. They simply find it difficult, if not impossible, to believe that actually some of the units simply marched the whole way, and that is having troops of the quality one does have.

HANRAHAN: A lot of speed depends on that skill and that ability to operate in those conditions?

81

MOORE: Indeed, and of course the speed with which our men, once they had the logistics to do so, were able to operate successfully in the mountains. You will have noticed that the thing went in fits and starts. Of course once an opportunity opens you must grab it and go. But having gone so far you then have got clearly to build up the necessary logistic backing to be able to undertake a battle, and the battle lasted, what, three nights in the hills just outside Stanley, so it obviously took a great deal of logistic backing before it could begin. You heard and witnessed a great deal of artillery fire going on, and that couldn't be done until we got the ammunition forward to do it.

HANRAHAN: Did you have the ammunition to go on firing? I mean, were you set for a longer exchange if need be?

MOORE: We had plenty of ammunition with the force to have gone on a long time, but any operation is a matter of judgement and we were having to balance the ability of our . . . even our extremely good and experienced troops – many of whom are Arctic-trained – to withstand the conditions in the mountains against having the ideal amount of ammunition to continue a battle for a very long time. As the Duke of Wellington said after Waterloo: 'It was a damn fine thing or a damn close-run thing'. Similarly here in some ways, this was a close-run thing in that batteries of guns which started that final night with 400 rounds a gun were down to as few as six, and that despite the helicopters flying all night trying to get the ammunition up.

HANRAHAN: What was it that produced that surrender? That collapse, it seems just to have happened?

MOORE: I've never witnessed an event like that before, but I joined the services after the end of the war. I've not witnessed such a thing and so I don't really think I could say what it is. It is obviously the collapse of will which is arrived at some point and I suppose in all major campaigns that one has come across. Through history there comes a point where there is a collapse of will and suddenly it spreads. It's astonishing the speed with which it spreads, isn't it? A fascinating morning that was. I'd just been up in the mountains with the two Brigadiers discussing what we were going to do next, and I'd given my orders and they were about to start the next phase, and suddenly there they were all over the hills, standing up and coming out of their holes and things, and we just stopped firing and held everything. It was a touch-and-go business because we had an air strike coming in and of course it was quite a difficult business to get to the pilots in the aeroplanes to hold it off, but suddenly they just weren't fighting any more, were they? Fascinating.

SUMMING UP
Brian Hanrahan: Tuesday 15 June

It's been a long and at times a dangerous journey getting there. But winning this battle has done nothing to solve the underlying problem. I've been talking to some of the Argentinian prisoners and they believe that these islands are Argentinian and they believe it passionately and sincerely. Equally, the Falkland Islanders I talked to have had their beliefs reinforced that they must remain British. It's a deadlock, but if these islands are to return to peace and tranquillity a long-term solution has got to be found.

There's now a major task of repair and reconstruction. As well as making everything safe the engineers are trying to return normal services to the people living in the town. Apart from the shattered water mains, the electricity cables have been brought down by the final hours of fighting. Even repairing the power cables was a slow affair, with men checking that booby-traps hadn't been left behind.

HOW MANY PRISONERS?

Brian Hanrahan: Wednesday 16 June

The British have now had a chance to count their prisoners, and found the number much smaller than the Argentinians had told them. 6200 men have been captured in Stanley and there are no more than 2000 on West Falkland. Other stragglers are still being rounded up but it seems unlikely there'll be more than 9000 of them. The original figure of nearly 15,000 was provided by the Argentinians, but subsequent investigation has shown that this claim – like many others they've made – has been exaggerated.

They've been queueing up in long lines to hand in their weapons and they're being mustered at the airfield. There is a problem finding shelter for them and the weather is as bad as it's ever been – cold, with regular downpours of rain. They're living in their own bivouacs: some have tents; others have built little sheds from the debris; others have dug themselves trenches and covered them with groundsheets. They're also using their own rations which are plentiful and, according to Major-General Jeremy Moore, the British commander, they may be getting better treatment than under their own officers. General Moore says the sooner they're away home the better as far as he's concerned, and they're already being loaded up on ships to take them away from the islands.

General Moore has also been praising the high quality of the soldiers fighting under him. He says their skill, determination and fighting efficiency are responsible for what in military terms are the relatively low level of British casualties. Thirty-three men died and 140 were injured in the final three-day battle for Port Stanley. The General said his men had gone in hard and got stuck in. If they'd held back the casualties would have been higher.

The army have now begun the major task of clearing up Port Stanley after the occupation; they're restoring power and water supplies, communications with London, and getting the airport runway fixed. But supplies are already arriving – a Hercules made an air drop this afternoon. The General said his men had been fighting for the islanders. The Argentinians had been fighting for the islands.

SENDING THE PRISONERS HOME (1)

Robert Fox: Wednesday 16 June

The last of the Argentinian soldiers have now left Port Stanley to hand in their weapons and equipment on the airfield, two miles out of town to the east. The 6-7000 prisoners from the Stanley area are to be embarked in the liner *Canberra* and the ferry *Norland,* to be shipped home to Argentina. The senior naval officer in charge, Commodore Michael Clapp, says that the navy is now dealing with a major disaster-relief programme. He's worried about conditions out on the airfield at Stanley, where there was a chill factor of minus 18 degrees centigrade overnight from the Antarctic wind. And many of the young soldiers have thin blankets and ragged jackets. They've been trying to make shelter in temporary bivouacs.

On West Falkland about 2000 men have surrendered. According to Commodore Clapp some were like skeletons. Their officers had let them starve, while other units were well fed. At Port Howard soldiers took bones from the dogs and ate the seed put down for the chickens.

The plan to return the Argentinians is being held up by the lack of response from the Argentinian authorities. The military commander on the Falklands, General Menendez, signed an unconditional surrender for all Argentinian forces on the islands. He has been allowed to contact General Galtieri from aboard HMS *Fearless,* but so far he has failed to agree to a full ceasefire involving all the mainland forces of Argentina, and for a safe passage for the ships bringing the prisoners back to Argentinian ports.

SENDING THE PRISONERS HOME (2)

Robert Fox: Friday 18 June

The news that *Canberra* is to sail direct to Argentina has brought an immense sense of relief. For many of the ship's company, and the embarked force, it could mean that peace might really arrive soon and all hostilities will be called off formally. The Senior Naval Officer aboard, Captain Burnham, and the ship's captain, Dennis Scott-Masson, say that Puerto Madryn is particularly suitable as it is a sheltered anchorage which could make the discharge of prisoners rapid, even if the *Canberra* is not allowed to go alongside in the port.

With the announcement of the fall of General Galtieri and the departure for Argentina, prisoners have looked much less tired. Marching to the ship they seemed dejected after the miseries of Stanley Airfield exposed to Antarctic gales. One group of prisoners said they wanted to give their two guards a present for looking after them so well. The return to Argentina has clearly put some of the professional officers and NCOs in a dilemma. They are courteous to their British counterparts, whereas ashore in Stanley many have been surly, refusing to accept that they were prisoners of war, and refusing to accept the defeat of the Argentine forces on the Falklands altogether. Now they have to go back to their homelands and face a public which had been ill-prepared to receive them and continuously misinformed of what has taken place on the Falklands and in the air and sea battles round them over the last six weeks.

SENDING THE PRISONERS HOME (3)
Robert Fox: Saturday 19 June

Once the procedure for disembarkation was agreed, Major Cariso, the senior officer among the prisoners, went ashore. There was a salute and a handshake from the Brigadier, and then the Major watched silently for more than an hour as his men clattered down the metal gangways to climb into lorries which took them to a nearby airbase. There were no crowds on the quay. Only about a hundred sailors and army and navy officers. There was little emotion, only a brief ripple of applause when the first group of officers appeared. One man wept as he embraced his son. But the rest had no relatives to greet them. The sick and wounded were taken on stretchers, some were on crutches, their feet swollen and black with frostbite and trench foot. Some of the P & O crew, like Frank and Anna Taylor, who had worked tirelessly in the wards, came to wave goodbye to the men they had nursed and made friends with. They have even thrown themselves on top of their patients during the worst air-raids to prevent further injury.

It has been a remarkable voyage for the *Canberra*. The first time she has berthed since 9 April when she left Southampton, and now the *Canberra* is making all speed to the Falklands, possibly to pick up another contingent of prisoners of war to be taken back home to Argentina.

CLEARING THE MINEFIELDS

Brian Hanrahan: Monday 21 June

Clearing the minefields is proving exceptionally hazardous. The mines are made of plastic, they contain no metal parts, and the army's mine detectors do not register them. The work is being done by commando-trained engineers crawling across the peat on their hands and knees, feeling beneath the surface of this with their fingers or metal probes.

Two of them have been badly injured in the week since hostilities ended. The minefields are at the outskirts of Stanley and spread down to the sea and up into the mountains. The Argentine army and the marines both laid mines without referring to each other. Sometimes there are remains of Argentine soldiers who were blown to pieces when they wandered into another unit's minefields.

And the records that were kept are inaccurate both about the location and the number of mines. Many were also laid on the beaches and have already shifted in the sands. In addition to the formal minefields, a large number of little anti-personnel mines were scattered across the hillsides by helicopter. Finding them all will be a long and chancy business.

IN MEMORIAM

Within days of the ceasefire a funeral service was held in Port Stanley for the three civilians who died in the final bombardment. Memorial services were held for the British servicemen who died at Goose Green and Bluff Cove.

FALKLAND CIVILIANS' FUNERAL

Brian Hanrahan: Thursday 17 June

The three women were the only civilians to die during the occupation. They were killed during the final stages of the battle, when a British shell hit a part of the town which it was thought was unoccupied. General Moore, the British commander, has already said that on this occasion he'd got it wrong, he was sorry. The General had 'flu and couldn't attend today's service, but he did send a representative. It was ecumenical, conducted by both Catholic and Anglican ministers, in the tiny cathedral. Several hundred islanders packed it, and pallbearers from the Royal Marines and the Paratroopers helped to carry the wooden coffins.

The Anglican minister, Harry Bagnall, offered the sympathy of the community to those who'd been bereaved, and said he was sure he spoke also for the armed forces who came to set them free. Afterwards, the Islands' senior administrator in the absence of the Governor, Harold Rowlands, said he was sure nobody would hold the British forces responsible for their deaths. The service had also been a time to remember the British troops who'd been killed and injured in the battle. He said: 'The world must know how grateful we are to the British who lost their husbands and sons fighting for us. The only word I can use is "thank you".'

WELSH GUARDS AT BLUFF COVE

Brian Hanrahan: Wednesday 23 June

The Welsh Guards formed up three sides of a square, looking over the rails towards *Sir Galahad*, still burning two weeks after the air attack. Among them were seamen from the Royal Fleet Auxiliary who manned the ships. The choir of the Welsh Guards opened the service with 'The Lord is my Shepherd', and then, after their Commanding Officer, Lieutenant-Colonel Rickett, had read a lesson, the Regimental Sergeant-Major read the list of those who died: a long, cold list – fifty names, thirty-eight of them Guardsmen, and then their cooks, their engineers, the doctors and their assistants who'd come to save life, and seven seamen who'd brought them there.

At the end a bugler played The Last Post, his notes uncertain – the cold wind had frozen his fingers and his lips. Then the chaplain gave a blessing to the ship, which will be towed out to sea to be sunk as a war grave: 'Go forth, Christian souls,' he said, 'on thy journey from this world.' On shore there's a single cross, and another to be erected by the people of the local settlement, Fitzroy. They wish to put up a plaque to remember those who died and create a garden around it. As the service ended, the flames aboard *Sir Galahad* could be seen flickering in the dusk, and the choir sang the Welsh National Anthem, 'Land of my Fathers'.

GOOSE GREEN AND DARWIN

Robert Fox: Friday 25 June

The simple iron cross was dedicated on a cold winter's afternoon by men representing all the units of the Battle of Goose Green – the Army Air Corps, the engineers, gunners and men of the Merchant Navy and Royal Navy were there too. The monument can be seen from both Darwin and Goose Green, and settlers from both chose the site and made the plinth of local stone. It represents the support of the local Falkland people, said the padre of the Second Battalion, Parachute Regiment, David Cooper. Without their support the whole thing would have been meaningless.

The simple inscription is to the memory of Lt-Col. H. Jones and all those who fell with him freeing the settlements on 28 May. There were a few prayers and two wreaths from the settlers. As the lesson was read by Major Chris Keeble, a patrol of Gurkhas marched back to Goose Green along the track by the shore. A flight of upland geese swept low across the water of the bay. A Gurkha bugler sounded Reveille and Last Post, and a Gurkha piper played the lament, the Flowers of the Forest, by the gully where H. Jones fell.

THE COMMUNICATIONS WAR

Throughout the Falklands war the media – newspapers as well as broadcasters – were in conflict with the Ministry of Defence about restrictions on the way that news was reported. After the ceasefire, Brian Hanrahan and Robert Fox expressed their own professional frustrations in the radio programme *From Our Own Correspondent*.

ON BEING A WAR CORRESPONDENT

Brian Hanrahan (TV): *From Our Own Correspondent*
Saturday 19 June

When I started on this assignment, the Ministry of Defence reached deep into its files and came up with a pile of greying forms printed in the fifties. They laid down the role of a war correspondent, told me that I was to be treated as an Army Captain, that I came under the orders of the Operational Commander, that I couldn't leave the battle zone without his permission, and was subject to military censorship. It also pointed out that the normal job of a correspondent was to publish information – the normal wish of the military was to keep it secret. It was a fair warning of the battles to come.

The first problem was to find a way of getting the information out. Almost as soon as we left Portsmouth the ship plunged into radio silence, and a broadcaster who can't talk is wasting his time. The written press fared a little better – the Navy has a satellite signalling system which, because the beams point up to the satellite, can't be picked up by direction-finding equipment on the ground. This could be used. Newspaper journalists could send their copy, but because they came at the end of a long queue of priority users, their material was getting to London late and there were severe limits on how much they could send. It was a recipe for some very frustrated journalists.

About a week out at sea, somebody discovered floating telephones. Many of the tankers and store ships had telephone and telex systems which also worked by satellite. They were available to us, but we had to get to them. The only way was by helicopter, and they were neither easily found nor easily flown in some of the weather we were going through. Quite often we had to be winched down in a rough sea, only to find ourselves stranded by bad weather or fog for days. The ships also had a distressing habit of heading in opposite directions and being out of helicopter range when the telephone call was finished. I very quickly learned to take a toothbrush when going to the telephone box. The problem was that, once on the store ship, although we had a telephone, we were cut off from information about what was happening, and

1 & 2 HMS *Invincible* leaves Portsmouth for the South Atlantic.

4

3 HMS *Hermes* sets sail from Portsmouth.
4 Brian Hanrahan (centre) with his camera team,
Bernard Hesketh (left) and John Jockel, aboard *Hermes*.
5 Marines practise disembarking from a Sea King helicopter
as it hovers over the deck of the *Hermes*.

6 The *General Belgrano* after being torpedoed by a
British submarine.
7 HMS *Sheffield* after being hit by an Exocet missile.

8 The frigate *Arrow* comes alongside to take off the crew of the *Sheffield*.
9 A survivor from the *Sheffield* arrives on *Hermes*.

10

11

12

13

10 British ships and helicopters in San Carlos Water.
11 Heavy equipment is brought ashore from a landing craft.
12 *Canberra*, showing the specially constructed helipads.
13 *Canberra*, looking more like a troopship than a luxury liner,
transfers troops in the Falklands.

14 & 15 HMS *Antelope* blows up and sinks.

Two casualties of 25 May. 16 HMS *Coventry*. 17 *Atlantic Conveyor*.

18 A captured Argentine soldier at Port San Carlos wears a
Royal Marine sweater.
19 Argentine prisoners captured at Goose Green.

20

21

20 Napalm bombs discovered at Goose Green.
21 A mass grave for thirty Argentine soldiers killed
at Darwin.
22 *Sir Galahad* burns as helicopters take off survivors.
23 Survivors from *Sir Galahad* are brought ashore.

24

25

24 Paras help wounded colleagues on Mount Longdon.
25 Argentine prisoners in Port Stanley are searched before being transferred to the airport.
26 Argentine soldiers line up to hand in their weapons outside Port Stanley.

27

28

27 Marines of 42 Commando
talk to residents as they
'house clear' Port Stanley.
28 Major-General Moore
with the Argentine surrender
document.

frustration was soothed only by the tolerant hospitality of the men of the Royal Fleet Auxiliary who manned the ships. They quite often found a bunch of bad-tempered itinerants camping on their floors for days on end.

The second problem was finding the time to work amidst all the business of surviving. On ship it was possible to shut out the threat of air-raids and go on writing; on land it just isn't. You go into a trench and you stay there for hours on end. You've also got to set up your own camp, cook your own food, and if necessary dig your own trench. It's a very time-consuming business, and in these cold and dangerous surroundings not one to skimp on. If travel between ships was difficult, on land it was a thousand times worse. There were no roads, and certainly not enough helicopters. Finding an empty helicopter to hitch a ride was a matter of asking every pilot in sight, sometimes waving one out of the sky. With that sort of logistical problem – days getting to a story, days getting back – it's easy to see how petty rows about censorship broke out.

But apart from the delayed copy and the cut-out words, there were deeper problems reflecting on the role of the free press. Bad news was instinctively delayed. When HMS *Sheffield* was lost the news was banned, and only later released in London under intense pressure. None of us wanted to tell that dreadful story, but it was important that it should come from the British side first. If Argentina had announced it first, only to have it confirmed by the British later, then every future Argentine claim would cause untold anguish at home. It's a principle that journalists hold to that accurate news should be released unimpeded. It strengthens the credibility of both the correspondent and the organisation he's reporting on. It's this ability to know the truth, even when it hurts, that we think sets democracies apart. Instead, we were faced with constant restraints and restrictions, which slowed and diminished our reporting. They seemed to have more to do with bureaucratic in-fighting in the Ministry of Defence than security. The fact that Vulcans had bombed Port Stanley was supposedly a state secret on one ship. On mine I was told it was an RAF matter and shouldn't be released through naval channels.

I don't think anyone objected to the censoring of military details which might help the enemy. After all, our lives were as much at risk as anybody else's. And with the local military command there were few difficulties. We did not report what they asked us not to. But the detailed censoring was left to civilian public relations men, whose instructions came from London and often seemed at odds with the local command. Sometimes the policy dictated from London seemed two-faced. While we withheld details of unexploded bombs, for the very good reason that Argentina might re-examine the fuses, highly accurate accounts were appearing in London newspapers, accounts which could only have come from within the Ministry of Defence. While we only reported past events, the attack on Darwin and the surrender of Goose Green were leaked before they happened. While we stayed silent about unopposed military advances, somebody announced in London that we were moving along the north coast long before there was evidence that the Argentinians had detected it.

So far, I've been talking in general terms about all journalism. But my particular job was reporting for television, and in television terms this is the unreported war. There is no doubt that military satellite-systems can carry television pictures, but no pictures have been sent – not even a test transmission has been authorised. It's hard to believe that no time in ten weeks could be found to show a little of what was happening, especially when world opinion was so important to Britain.

ON BEING A WAR CORRESPONDENT

Robert Fox (Radio): *From Our Own Correspondent*
Saturday 19 June

'Well, I suppose you could say this is really the radio man's war,' said my learned colleague from the *Standard,* Max Hastings, reciting a litany of his experiences in covering wars in Vietnam and the Middle East. In some ways he was right, in others quite wrong. For the radio man seeking that precious voice link to London from Goose Green, San Carlos, Teal Inlet or Stanley itself, much of the campaign has passed in a whirl of hitching lifts in helicopters, seizing boats to ply to stormy anchorage off San Carlos, of impersonating all ranks, high and low, to get the vital transfer to the ship with the right kind of satellite telephone to make the call to Broadcasting House. Communication, the mechanics and message, soon became an obsession.

In a tightly-knit community such as the British Falklands force, there soon develops a private language, a complete vocabulary, unintelligible to outsiders. Sometimes communications within a unit seem to break down altogether. A remarkable feature of the whole campaign was the amount of walking across the island, and two units, 3 Para and 45 Commando, virtually walked the breadth of East Island, some fifty miles, to line up for the assault on Stanley. The column of march of 45 would be some two miles long, and routine orders and messages would be passed from man to man, not over the radio. One damp afternoon the message came down 'Air-raid warning, Red'. And as the leaders got down in hollows and behind rocks, they saw the men bringing up the rear a mile away jumping up and throwing their rifles in the air, and the echo of 'Air-raid warning, Red' came back as 'Galtieri's dead, Hurray'.

Some of the words of the British fighting units have been hard to interpret to an outside audience. The feeling of grief and pride by 2 Para after the death of Colonel 'H' Jones and seventeen of their colleagues at Goose Green; the half-hour hiding under the gorse bushes outside Darwin, seemingly a lifetime under the plastering from mortar and ground-fired anti-aircraft fire; the care and dedication of the doctors and regimental medical orderlies to their wounded and dying, sometimes under fire – it is hard to describe aptly. In cold print it looks like a cliché.

Quite apart from trying to sort out the emotional and and linguistic algebra of such scenes and events, to make them intelligible to an audience 8000 miles away, there has been the technical poser of how physically to transmit the material to London. In this the twin talismans have been the helicopters and an instrument known as the Marisat

Satellite Communications System, which gives a clearer telephone call to London from a ship at San Carlos than a phone booth in Bognor or Brighton. In all hours of daylight, the Marines, Army and Navy pilots in their helicopters ferried casualties, ammunition and the odd journalist, and in that order, I hope, across some of the most difficult flying terrain. A few hours after the surrender at Goose Green, a Scout helicopter came to whisk me away to San Carlos. Once in the cockpit, the pilot said over the head-set, 'I haven't got a co-pilot today, mate. Give us a shout if you see any Pucara aircraft trying to shoot us up.'

Once safely returned to the San Carlos anchorage, other hazards loomed. Sometimes the ship with the right satellite had put to sea, and telex messages had to be written laboriously in block capitals by hand for the cryptographer to telex to the Ministry of Defence to be passed on to Broadcasting House. The representatives of the Ministry of Defence, both local and in London, became, as the campaign developed, an obstacle course for the unwary journalist in themselves.

On the other side, I am left with the enduring pleasure, the puzzlement, of the special language – a delight and danger – as one moved from one unit to another. The Paras 'Banjoed' Goose Green; the Marines 'Wellied' the positions on Mount Harriet; and the SAS 'Maletted' everything in sight. Depending on the circumstances, if it was 'Wasser' everything was going wonderfully, or terribly badly. But communication? Whether my colleagues and I have expressed to you adequately the drama, the rare pleasures, the terror and pain, the acts of selflessness and the sheer humanity in this strange and remote campaign, about this I must remain agnostic. I know one of my greatest crises of communication came the night after the Battle of Goose Green. Huddling in thin combat clothes, wondering whether my brain could keep my big toe in contact long enough to stave off frostbite. But then, I always was a hypochondriac.

LOOKING BACK FROM LONDON

The two correspondents have been ceaselessly busy since they returned to London shortly after the recapture of the Falklands had been completed. Hanrahan gave a long radio interview to Gordon Clough before setting to work on the TV series *Task Force South*; Fox has contributed to many radio programmes and has written a series of articles for *The Listener*.

LOOKING BACK

Brian Hanrahan: *From Our Own Correspondent*
Saturday 26 June

GORDON CLOUGH: Brian, could we, as it were, begin at the end when you left Port Stanley not very many days ago. We've heard about the devastation, in a sense – the lack of water, the lack of electricity, the amount of damage that was done inside houses (some houses themselves destroyed towards the end). What were conditions like when you left?

HANRAHAN: Well, they were coming back to normal quite rapidly. The major problem at that stage was the lack of services, and the lack of accommodation, so there were troops in everybody's houses – all over the place, sleeping in all the sheds. But they were beginning to get people off and on to ships and that was reducing the drain on the services. They were severely overloading both the electricity and the water supplies, and that was the major problem. People were beginning to resume their lives. Sheep were being brought in for slaughter, the roads were getting tidier, the mud was getting removed from them, the grass was growing along the verge, which they tell me was something that a little smart town like Port Stanley doesn't normally have, and they were pointing this out with utter horror to me that it was allowed to become so untidy. And the debris was being cleared away. Insides of the houses were still a bit dirty, but people were moving in, clearing up, coming back from the outer parts. Remember, there were only about 400 people out of a normal population, something like 1000, during the occupation, and people were beginning to drift back. But they were being discouraged from coming back and starting the job of cleaning up until there were fewer troops there and there was more accommodation available to them, and it was a far less dangerous place, because they were having to go through. They were finding ammunition stuffed in everywhere and there was always the risk that some of it was booby-trapped. Certainly, some of it had been going off for unexplained reasons, and they are fairly sure that these were booby-traps – in fact, one or two delayed-action timers were found, and I believe examples of them were brought back to London on the plane I came with, so that they can be analysed here to make sure that proper countermeasures could be worked out.

CLOUGH: There is, of course, I believe, anxiety still about the minefields around. How badly are those restricting movement?

HANRAHAN: Within the town there's no problem. It's perfectly safe. But outside it, it really is dangerous everywhere. The minefields themselves are marked on Argentine maps, but those maps have proven to be very inadequate because people were putting minefields down where they weren't supposed to, other units were laying minefields on top of minefields and not telling people. They do go up into the mountains. Up in the mountains there aren't formal minefields. There are masses of booby-traps left by the troops as defensive positions around their positions. There are also, I believe, lots of mines. I was warned to watch out in the mountains for mines which had just been thrown out of the helicopters. If they sink down into the turf, you'll never see them and they'll be almost impossible to find. So it's quite important to get up there and find them. But there are a lot of mines. They thought were were something like 15,000 mines laid around the area.

CLOUGH: Let me take you back now to the day ten, eleven weeks ago, when you were suddenly whipped off the top of the Television Reporters' rota and sent to *Hermes*. How did the atmosphere in the Task Force change as the fleet steamed south and you began to be more and more aware that something was going to happen?

HANRAHAN: It was a very slow change. To begin with, it was another exercise. And then it began to dawn on them (and on us) – and I think it was a slow realisation for all of us – that we might need to take this one a bit seriously, that these weren't just exercises, they were working up to something that might be real. And then very, very slowly the mood changed. People got a bit grimmer – began to

101

think about it more. But I still don't think anyone realised it was likely to turn into a shooting war until after we'd gone past Ascension. At that stage they started laying out the live armaments. And all the normal rules about what you do with live armaments just had to be thrown away. They'd been already stored rather oddly because there just wasn't time to obey the rules. But then they were out on the deck, they were all mixed up together, sitting there, pointing in the wrong directions, because if you were loading and unloading quickly you couldn't carefully stack them. That's when I think it began to hit. And of course, when we finally got down there and the first air-raid started, I think all their stomachs knotted up. It was the most horrifying noise. I'm sure that anybody who went through the last war and knows what it was like will think that I'm being foolish. But I know that my stomach knotted because I'd never heard anything like it, and it was the realisation that somebody out there was trying to kill me. And I think everybody went through the same sudden change of mind and everybody tensed up. And then *Sheffield* was hit.

CLOUGH: *Sheffield* was hit by the Exocet. Now, there seems to have been a bit of a feeling here that maybe the Navy had underestimated the Exocet. That the defence systems weren't really ready to cope with it.

HANRAHAN: I don't think anybody knew what an Exocet could do. In fact that goes for nearly every weapon – ours, theirs, all the missiles. They're completely untested in warfare. Lots of exercises had been done, lots of range firings. But no one had known, if it came to it, if someone got up there and we put all our anti-missile, anti-aircraft defences up, and they put all their evasion devices, or whatever they're called, electronic warfare bits together, and the two met head-on in a genuine clash, with everybody trying everything to get through and get at the other side. Not a controlled exercise when you do certain things – but for real. The *Sheffield* was a sneak attack – it just came in low. Flat sea, coming in under the radar. It came in, it had a very good pilot, very low level, quiet day, and sneaked in. Now, the systems didn't pick it up. It came in.

Delivered its weapon. When it comes to that, I don't think anybody knew what was going to happen. All sorts of old lessons relearnt. After a while, the ships' superstructures were covered with machine-guns, because it was realised that all the modern methods were cutting a swathe out of the sky, you couldn't fly between x feet and y feet (and that went up a long, long way) because our missile systems were too good. On the other hand, if you came in low enough you could defeat them. So what they were trying to do was come in low, and slow enough in order to be able to deliver it accurately from a low-level attack, at which point they became vulnerable to machine-guns. So suddenly we had machine-guns everywhere, and they were shooting things down. And that shouldn't happen. You shouldn't be able to shoot down fast modern fighters that can go at supersonic speeds with machine-guns. But they do, and they did, and I think other people in the world – the Israelis, I believe, learned that lesson long before – but what happens is you use your modern weapons to make no-go areas and then you go back to the old-fashioned way to clear out anything that is within range.

CLOUGH: When people saw what had happened to *Sheffield* – heard what had happened to *Sheffield* – was the worry that was expressed here about the construction of those ships reflected in the fleet?

HANRAHAN: Entirely so. There was a very strong feeling that the modern hulls – all the modern hulls – just weren't built the way old ones were. They had more aluminium in them, that made them . . . they melted at about half the temperature. I think it's 700 or something degrees centigrade that aluminium melts at – steel is 1500 – and therefore once a fire started – with an aluminium hull, or a greater proportion of aluminium above the waterline, it could spread much more quickly, and it did. There are other things about design too. The difference between *Hermes* and *Invincible*. *Hermes* is a brute of a ship to live on. It has doors everywhere, it has pipes everywhere, you were constantly brushing past them and squeezing through spaces.

It is not designed for living in at all. It's a very

old-fashioned ship, laid down at the end of the last war in the days when ships were functioning objects and no one wasted much time in making them pretty. But it's a tough ship, and everyone felt that, and the Captain certainly did, that if it got hit, it was going to survive. Not only was it going to survive but it was going to fight. And he was working on the basis that, even if he got hit by an Exocet and he lost some of his crew and part of the ship, he was going to make that ship go on and be a viable aircraft-carrier, capable of sustaining its role, which was to defend the rest of the fleet. I know the Captain of *Invincible* had precisely the same intention, but his ship is a newer ship. It has wide passageways, it has bulkheads which are further apart, I don't know what its hull construction is. But you could see instantly the difference between one which was built with no thought for comfort, but built purely to be a fighting machine; and the other one which was built on more modern lines and, I dare say, with economy in mind as well, because they've become fiercesomely expensive. How much it's going to cost to replace all those that are lost, I shudder to think.

CLOUGH: It's curious, isn't it, that the older ships seem to be the better able to resist the most modern missiles? I'm thinking of *Glamorgan*, which I think was hit by an Exocet and survived?

HANRAHAN: Yes, *Glamorgan*. I saw the picture of it. And I was talking to one of the survivors – a man who had been injured in it, and he rather proudly pulled out a picture of *Glamorgan*, an aerial picture someone had given him, and there in the back was a huge hole. I mean, it had gone in at the back end, it had blown the flight-deck apart, it had blown up the hangar, it had killed five or six men – the flight crew – but the ship itself had gone away at full speed with all its systems working – it had taken an Exocet and survived, and really not suffered that much.

CLOUGH: Brian, I think we ought to move off now from the purely naval operation to the beginning of the land operation. But before we go on to the actual assault at San Carlos, a lot of speculation about the, as it were, pre-attack role of the SAS and SBS. Now, what were they doing?

HANRAHAN: They were on shore. They were carrying out, and we were forbidden flatly to talk about it at the time, but I don't think anyone minds now – they were carrying out very much a pure intelligence-gathering role. One of their leaders said to me it was like the first man going ashore. It's like putting a foot on the moon, you just didn't know what was going to happen – you didn't know the quality of the enemy, you didn't know where they were, how they were deployed, and how capable they were of catching you. Once you had your first party on shore, they then started sending back radio. Once you had your first party on shore, they then started sending back radio. And I used to watch the men from the signals, sitting up on the top deck with their equipment, listening in to the reports coming in from ashore. No one would say what they were doing, or why, but they were getting reports in from their scouting parties.

CLOUGH: How far ahead of the actual landing was this?

HANRAHAN: It's hard to be precise. I'm told that the first of them were on shore something like a month before the other troops.

CLOUGH: Good heavens! Were they working in co-operation with the islanders, were they being helped?

HANRAHAN: No. No, they were given orders to stay away from the islanders because (1) they would stick out. I mean you could actually get a roll of the islanders and you'd spot strangers amongst them. And (2) it was feared that it would jeopardise the islanders, and the islanders talking amongst themselves might well jeopardise the special forces. So they were told: Stay up on the hills. And in fact, some of them apparently stayed up there a month, living wild in that country with no cover, and having to remain completely out of sight of everybody. And just sticking their radios up and sending off messages. And gradually they fed back information about where the enemy were, what their units were, what strength they were deployed. More and more SAS/SBS were able to get ashore, and they built up a picture of what it was like on the island.

CLOUGH: Clearly information of great value to the Task Force Commander when he was planning his operation at San Carlos. Now, what was that like? You were there. You were with the ships in the Sound, when it turned from 'bomb alley' into 'death alley' for the Argentine air force.

HANRAHAN: It really was very scary because we had almost no defences. The ships out in the Sound were doing the defending, and they took heavy losses. I think almost everything that was out in the Sound.

CLOUGH: It was the intensity of that air attack, I think, that made people wonder whether it was wise to take *Canberra* in and then leave her there for so long.

HANRAHAN: Yes, I think there were a lot of changes of mind about that. *Canberra* was going to go in, she wasn't going to go in, and then she was going to go in. The advantage of *Canberra* was that you could get in all the troops in one very swift movement. I think that, in retrospect, everyone would agree it was probably a mistake to leave her there. Once having discharged her troops she should have moved out. But then that was a general thing. A lot of ships which were in there on the first day after that amazingly intense air-raid . . . Everybody pulled out. There were a few ships left in, a couple of store ships unloading. But the rest of the fleet pulled out. They left a warship or two to protect those that were there, and to let the missile systems settle down. Because one of the discoveries of this is that the Rapier, which is a very effective box of tricks which was doing amazingly good work towards the end, takes time to settle in. Its gyroscopes, its operators need to get their eye in, and these lads had been given something like one missile a year to fire in practice, because they are so expensive, and suddenly, there they are, firing them off left, right and centre, and they just had to get used to the system.

CLOUGH: Was this part of the problem at Bluff Cove when *Sir Galahad* was so disastrously hit, and *Tristram*? There was worry that there wasn't air cover there. Was that because the carriers were too far away, or . . .?

HANRAHAN: No, the system was air-covered because they put the Harriers in later in the day to reassure everybody that it was there. They were cruising backwards and forwards above us. I mean – too late – but the system that was being operated was that there was a free-fire zone above the ships. At that stage the Rapier had only just been installed that day, the ships that brought it were the ones that were hit. It had only been got off and it only just about started to settle down. They did get a couple of shots off, but the system hadn't stabilised enough to be effective. And on top of that, it was a very, very good air strike. Because they came in without any warning. We did not have the radar cover to detect aircraft coming in, and I personally, and I have nothing to back it up, but I'm personally quite convinced it was a directed air strike. We know there were Argentine observation posts in the mountains. On that particular day, the cloud cover had cleared and they were able to see down – they could have seen the ships, and undoubtedly, I think, that strike was a directed strike at a precise target, and it paid off for the Argentinians.

CLOUGH: Still, the tragedy of *Sir Galahad* brings me on to what I think is rather a sensitive area. There have been reports from some reporters – not, I think, from you – of a certain resentment among the army and the marines of the way the navy handled itself. People saying Admiral Woodward deserves the Burma Star because his ships were so far to the East; there are reports of friction between the Admiral and the General. Is that true? You must have met them both and talked to them. Do you feel that there's anything that could have been more easily handled?

HANRAHAN: I think they're both far too cautious as men to admit things like that to me. I haven't been back out since the end of hostilities to the navy, I mean to talk to the Task Force people. There's certainly hostility on the ground towards the navy's being so distant. I think that is ill-informed criticism. The prime role of the Task Force Commander at sea was to keep his aircraft-carriers safe. And his ships were there to defend the route in, to keep the skies clear, and to keep air cover up, and the only air cover in the first few days had to come from the Harriers, and if they hadn't been there it would undoubtedly have been a great deal worse. He was putting a lot of Harriers up, there were limits to how long they could remain on station, and I think to accuse him of being cowardly, as I believe has been said, would be totally wrong. His job was to ensure that that cover continued. There is, I know, also a second level of criticism which is a technical one, and I think that the cowardice charges are really a more popular version of those, but I know there is a technical argument that says it is possible for the Task Force ships to have come in closer, to have applied themselves in different formations, thereby being able to give better, closer air cover (because the problem with operating at a distance if you keep your carriers back on the extreme Argentine air-raid range to defend them, you give your aircraft less time on station over the island itself). There is an argument that says they could have been brought in closer, that would have exposed them to air attack, but by deploying the forces differently, that could have been countered. I am unable, literally, to understand it, and I think there's also an element of, shall I say, 'theory' about this, and there has been a lot of theory flying around, and what actually has mattered in the last few weeks has been practice. You can draw curves on the graph for ever which say 'this is what should happen'. But we've seen example after example when things that shouldn't happen did happen, and the other way round.

CLOUGH: Brian, there's obviously a great deal more we could talk about the fighting, but one thing that has been of concern to us, working in London, and you, working in the South Atlantic, has been the criticism of the BBC for various things. As far as you're concerned, the World Service broadcasts being accused of making life a good deal harder, for instance, at Goose Green. How strong was the feeling that the BBC had been offending in some way?

HANRAHAN: The resentment against the BBC was immense. I think I'd enjoyed quite good relationships with most people until then, and for a week afterwards everybody I met told me what they thought of me. And I could explain till I was blue in the face that the BBC hadn't invented the information, it'd been given it, and it was published information. It didn't make any difference – the BBC was the purveyor of it. Gradually that mood swung round to realising that the information had come from London. It caused enormous resentment, and I think there is considerable anger still amongst most of the officers, who want a lot of things looked at, as to the amount of information that was released in London which they considered to be sensitive. Another very small example, not a very small example, a very important example, but it illustrates the point. Unexploded bombs. We had a complete blackout on talking about unexploded bombs, and yet I picked up a London newspaper several weeks later which was sent out to us, and there, on the day that *Antelope* had blown up, was a complete story explaining how a very gallant man had lost his life trying to defuse a bomb which had hit it. That caused anger. No one was supposed to talk about it. It may have been obvious that there were some bombs that weren't going off, but there were a lot that didn't go off. Bombs were coming down all over the place. All sorts of ships were hit by bombs that didn't go off. Now, a lot of effort and time . . . Both *Galahad* and *Lancelot* were hit by bombs that didn't go off, and about a week was spent getting those bombs out and throwing them over the side. And the stories of the men who did it are tremendous stories. But we were keeping them quiet because for strategic reasons nobody wished to give away this fact, and yet it was being leaked in London. For good reasons, they wanted to pay tribute to the man who'd died. But it was felt that that really should not have happened at that stage.

CLOUGH: One very striking thing in the film of yours that we saw last night was your saying that you'd talked to a lot of Argentine prisoners, and you'd talked to Falkland islanders, and from what the two sides had said to you, you were convinced that this wasn't the end of it.

HANRAHAN: It's not the end of the problem. Judging by the reaction of the prisoners. They said that these are their islands. There has got to be a solution – we don't want you here. The people who live there are totally convinced that they are British islands and this has reinforced it. They have no desire to live under anything Argentinian – even remotely so. They might have considered it. Several people said to me that if the Argentinians had gone on with their gentle tactics of wooing for a few more years, people might have got used to them. They were slowly beginning to achieve their ends. But there's a complete reversal there now – nobody there would accept it. I don't know what you do. Men have lost their lives now – both sides. Without judging the claims, the sincerity of belief on both sides is such that it's hard to see how it can be resolved.

CLOUGH: I think it would be improper of me not to end by saying, from Radio News, anyway, thank you to you and to your crew, to Bernard Hesketh and John Jockel, for the amazing work you've done.

HANRAHAN: I think those two in particular, who have taken, I think, rather greater risks than I, because they had to stand there in the middle of everything and film, have been quite heroic. And equally, while I may have been staggering around with a pack on my back – nothing like the pack that the soldiers were carrying – they carried something like about 100 pounds of equipment each over those mountains – while I may have been staggering about under my pack, they were staggering about under bigger packs full of technical gear, and carrying cameras and recorders and all the paraphernalia needed to run video – modern, high-quality video equipment – up in freezing cold mountains, and to repair it if it'd gone wrong, and they did it, and they did it uncomplainingly for weeks on end. I don't know how they did it.

CLOUGH: Perhaps it's a bit early to ask you this, and perhaps it's a bit too personal – but how do you think you've been changed by this?

HANRAHAN: I'm not sure I do know. I mean, I literally fell off a flight last night. I think I've thought a bit more, and I won't go much further than that, about what I think is right and proper, and about what matters. And about using my time. There's nothing like thinking you haven't got a lot of it to wonder if perhaps you should do what you want to do when you get the chance and not wait and think about doing it next year or the year after – do it now.

RETURN HOME

Robert Fox: *From Our Own Correspondent* Friday 2 July

In the past few weeks the inner and outer harbours at Stanley and Port William have seen more ships riding at anchor than since the First World War. There have been the ferries and the liner *Canberra*, the frigates and amphibious warfare ships *Intrepid* and *Fearless*, the rusty trawlers now serving as minesweepers, bravely flying the white ensign. Between them there has been the monotonous buzz of commuting small boats, tugs, lifeboats, and the small launches – the growlers. Above, the clatter of helicopters dangling artillery pieces brought in from the hills, and nets of supplies and ammunition. Landing craft ply between the rickety public jetty and the *Canberra* and the *Norland* with the lucky para battalions and marine commandos now on their way home. In the mud of Port Stanley, the Gurkhas and the Scots and Welsh Guards have moved in to take up garrison duties. As their salute to the people the Pipe Band of the Scots Guards paraded along the shore road to Government House and back to the jetty, the wail of the pipes drowned by the helicopters in the gathering dusk.

The mood of the troops that fought for Port Stanley has changed from battle readiness to the more languid tempo of garrison life, of the relaxation of the journey home. Outwardly there is little sign of battle fatigue. In the hospital, now manned by military as well as civilian doctors, there are signs of exhaustion on the faces of those who have worked night and day after the air-raids, the attacks on Goose Green and mountains west of Stanley, helping the hundreds of injured and maimed. But 'winding down' is more a question of changing a habit of mind than just physical relaxation. For the civilians of us who followed General Moore's forces from San Carlos into Stanley it also means a complete change of vocabulary.

Military jargon seemed booby-trapped; it varied considerably from unit to unit. Marines talk about 'scran' for food, army units eat 'scoff'. The divergence in lingo seems to reflect the different approach to soldiering. The paras are light assault troops, and once engaged like to move fast to gain the objective; the marines appear more methodical in their build-up, perhaps a product of their nautical training. Sometimes the language barrier threatened operations. In the landing at San Carlos a company of paras arrived at the beach in a landing craft driven by Royal Marines. Once the ramp went down the marine sergeant said correctly, 'Troops Out'; the paras just stared at the dark water they were being invited to jump into up to their waists. The order was repeated twice. Then a sergeant major gave the parachute jumping order 'Go' and the men charged up the beach.

Listen to any routine radio conversation by units in the field and you find as thick a disguise to plain language as the sticky camouflage cream we all had to wear by courtesy of Max Factor. It is all about locating 'sunray' and 'hawkeye' or getting the 'shelldrake' and the 'starlight' – these are the commanding officer, a helicopter, the artillery officer and the doctor. Within a matter of weeks or even days the new slang becomes a habit. I was talking to an Argentinian aboard *Canberra*, a Welsh Patagonian called Milton Rhys from Trelew, who said shyly: 'I have to go now to get some scoff.' The para guards reciprocated with slogans such as 'Putto el rubbisho in el baggo por favore rapido'.

Beside the language barrier, there was the time warp. It was not just that this appeared to be a very old-fashioned expedition, the last piece of gunboat diplomacy of the Empire, covered only by British journalists. There was also the fact the Navy had to do everything in Zulu; or in other words the Navy insisted on working to Greenwich Mean Time, Zulu time as it's known. This was three hours behind local time and four behind Port Stanley. Different ships worked to different times. *Canberra* always used local time. So you could fly in a helicopter round Stanley harbour and get jet-lag. I left *Canberra* at breakfast to arrive at *Fearless* ten minutes later for lunch.

But in Port Stanley, now preparing for a garrison of about three times its population, tricks of the clock or language cannot disguise the effects of battle, shock and fatigue. Some of the gutted houses look like Paul Nash war paintings. The streets are muddy and broken. On the beaches and the hills there are mines, many undetectable. For the Kelpers, the islanders, there is little prospect of moving back in time to the freedom and easy-going life of the days before the Argentinian invasion, little prospect of 'winding down' or finding another home to go to.

THE RAT-PACK WAR

Robert Fox: *The Listener* Thursday 8 July

The Upland Goose Hotel in Port Stanley has little in common with the Intercontinentals, Commodores, Hiltons and Ledra Palaces which have been the press centres of so many of the media wars of the last two decades. And I am sure the proprietors, Mr and Mrs Desmond King and family, will not mind me saying so. But it did come to serve the same function as the home of the itinerant hacks after the Argentine surrender on 14 June. Though short on telex, television, telephone and all other communication aids, barring carrier pigeon, there was hot water after three days, intermittent electricity supply and good home cooking. In style, architecture and hospitality it had all the familiarity of the comfortable hotels of the West Country I grew up in; but this was a style as foreign to the taste of most of the city-bred fellow newsmen as Peking duck, nasi goreng and tagliarini al pesto.

Despite the fact that the affair was utterly British, British troops and sailors fighting for a British colony and reported entirely by British press, to most of the journalists, myself included, there was something utterly exotic

113

about the Falklands winter campaign. It was the rat-pack war. I do not mean that the newsmen behaved like a collective of rodents; far from it. We were divided up into small groups, often with individuals following one unit, and did not see one another for days or even weeks on end. When I say 'rat-pack', I am borrowing the military abbreviation for 'rations pack', which we lived on solidly (the *mot juste* in the case of biscuits AB and AB Fruit and compo paste) for days and weeks in the field. There was a small choice. First, you had either 'rats Arctic' or 'rats GS (General Service)', with a further variation between menu 'A' and menu 'B', which meant either dehydrated chicken supreme or curry. According to the gourmets, the Arctic rats were better, but needed much more water, fine for Arctic snows, not so good in the Falklands where the perils of liver fluke lurked in many of the streams.

Mastery of cooking and constructing trench, 'basher' or 'bivvy' shelter in the open were among the first obligations for anyone intending to march with General Moore's men into Stanley. A whole new range of skills and language had to be acquired along with camouflage trousers and smocks, Arctic socks and underwear and, as clinging as Falklands peat mud, camouflage cream, courtesy of Max Factor. Integration with the forces was not easy. When first I put on smock and trousers, puttees and boots I was greeted by one of the sergeants of 2 Para, Phil Atkinson, with the accolade: 'You are the most unmilitary-looking person I have met in my life. My eight-year-old daughter could do better than you.' With the clothes and rations came a crash course in battle first-aid and survival in the open, and a new vocabulary. It became a world of 'yomping' and 'tabbing' (walking), 'proffing' (acquisition by less than legal means), 'rassing' (much the same but from the naval RAS–Replenishment at Sea), 'hacking it' (i.e. achieving it), and 'oppos' (i.e. your mates). 'If you think you are getting frostbite, stick your toes in your oppo's crutch,' was the injunction of Sergeant Pennington, an ex-SAS survival expert, 'it's the warmest part of his body and that's your best chance.' The name of the game was to show that you could 'hack it'. Gradually distance turned to trust, and in the end a strange friendship. A week after landing at San Carlos the 2 Para

114

RSM, Malcolm Simpson, showed me his new 'basher' with pride, a carefully-built three-star job made of rock sangar, trench and poncho roof with bracken in the camouflage net, worthy of mention in dispatches at the next Ideal Home Exhibition.

He never used it: that night he set out on a 'tab' for Goose Green. The next time I met RSM Simpson was when we were together being 'brassed up' by enemy artillery and mortar on the approach to Port Darwin. It was the first time I had been under such intense attack, and also, I discovered, it was the first time for him. Throughout the day we dived for the same cover, and discussed on equal terms the problems facing him, of handling the prisoners, tending the wounded, getting up ammunition, and wrapping up the dead. It was a temporary fellowship that will leave its imprint for life.

For all the tales of the horrors of war, the moments of real fear were comparatively short-lived, as were the days and nights of discomfort from the weather. At San Carlos the air strikes were sudden and lasted barely a few minutes. At Darwin and Goose Green the mortar and artillery and machine-gun fire grew to a crescendo in periods of about half an hour only at a time, mortar and artillery shrapnel crunching and pinging overhead less than a few feet away, white phosphorus shells bursting in the peat like giant fireworks as dawn approached. Sometimes there were moments of total surprise. On the day before the surrender, on a glorious sunny winter's morning, I was reading a letter from my brother, waiting to take a helicopter at Brigade Headquarters in the mountains above Estancia, when we were surprised by a Skyhawk attack. I saw the small bombs float to the ground, held by white parachutes, a mere thirty or forty yards away, twice over. A flash and shower of peat sod – and the only injury was superficial blast to an airman and perforated eardrums. The curse of the marathon marches across East Falkland, the peat bog, had been our friend. The ground was so soft that it soaked up the impact of bomb, bullet and mortar.

The cold became a threat only rarely: worst was when the packs and the down-filled Arctic sleeping-bags were not brought forward. This happened after the battle above

Darwin, and it was only the generosity of three paras, who allowed me to roll up with them in ponchos and water-proofs, that saved my toes that night. Those who wanted to march and live with the marines and the paras had to be prepared if not to die, to suffer at least trench foot, hunger and lack of sleep with them. Accordingly, primitive skills were quickly acquired, such as learning to keep one pair of socks dry, and tying the damp ones inside your trousers or putting them in your crutch at night to dry them for the morning.

It was something of a surprise, then, to hear a colleague pontificating on the *Today* programme about life in the wild and the necessity of keeping wet socks on your feet at night – one of the short cuts to trench foot. The reporting of the winter campaign has hardly brought forth any flowers of the New Journalism. Perhaps we have all been corrupted by the telethons of Vietnam television reporting and what *Reader's Digest* used to call the 'first person approach', which more recent electronic and press reporters have cultivated in mini-wars from Cyprus to El Salvador. For one that has worked in the Cinderella broadcasting medium, radio, for nearly fifteen years, it was fascinating to see how the frustrated television reporters were drawn to radio reporting of the expedition with all the pangs and passions of puppy love. For the ITN reporters, at least, the Marisat telephone became Narcissus' pool.

Others took a more robust view of the task. Mr Max Hastings, *Standard, Express* and *Spectator*, plus guest radio appearances, tried to emulate the strictures for such coverage laid down by Lord Copper and the *Daily Beast* in *Scoop*, churning out editorials, commentaries and reports, in that order of priority, like an old-fashioned sausage machine. His grasp of communications and sense of where to be for a final action was better than any, which won him no favours and house points with the rest of the pack. But the *Sunday Express* boast that 'only two names have dominated the Falklands war, Galtieri and Max Hastings,' hardly does them and their reporter credit, and seems to cover a rather narrow political spectrum. Stranger still the pirouettes of the *Daily Express*, which, after the apparent triumphalism with which they covered the fighting, seem to be going in for some good, old-fashioned 'knocking copy'. The quality Sundays know what the real stuff of investigation is about, and initially went into the general shenanigans of the various inter-staff bickerings and cock-ups with the enthusiasm they generally reserved for a police corruption case in Batley.

The world of the Falklands campaign was so enclosed that it was hard not to identify with the troops on the ground; in the heavier engagements it was the only means of psychological survival. But because of the campaign's remoteness and its almost parochial Britishness there will be a tendency for some time to come, I suspect, for the prints and TV to lurch from 'the paper that backs our boys' to 'the rag that slags the lads'. To start fluttering fans because troops fired on each other in the dark in the Falklands, which they did tragically on three occasions to my knowledge, strikes me as absurd. How many times can this have happened in Vietnam, Northern Ireland, Korea and Europe in the last war. I remember asking the *Express* reporter about the first such engagement above Port San Carlos the weekend of 22-23 May, to get the record straight. 'It is not the sort of thing we like to mention here,' said the man pompously. Yet I find he makes an 'exclusive' revelation of this on the front page of the *Express* for Friday 2 July.

Much of the copy when it found its way back to the Fleet and the Land Force did annoy, and the role of the press was certainly not to act as public relations men for the military, though they badly needed some, judging by the job done by the Ministry's PROs with the Force. Working for the World Service made life particularly tricky at times. Programmes and bulletins were being listened to by someone in a signals tent somewhere all the time. Often it was the review of what the London papers were reporting that raised the temperature. But, on the whole, I found a remarkable sensibility and sense of discrimination between the organisation, what it had to report, and individuals representing the BBC in the field, i.e. myself and Brian Hanrahan. After the Goose Green surrender, I was 'rassing' a cup of tea, or 'brew', from the Ajax Bay hospital at about midnight. The injured from the battle, mostly Argentines, were still pouring in, terribly maimed and burnt. Flight Lieutenant Swann, leader of the RAF Bomb Disposal Team, was particularly upset about a news item or press review reported on the BBC about the number of Argentine bombs not exploding due to poor fusing or delivery too low. After this, he said, they had started using French retard bombs and ten men had been killed behind the hospital when ammunition went up at Ajax, and Blue Beach at San Carlos was hit at the same time. 'Don't blame this one, mate,' said the large, bearded figure of Commander Rick Jolly, the executive surgeon of the hospital, 'he's been at the Goose Green punch-up. It's probably one of those civil servants again leaking it to the defence correspondents, just to show they're in on the act and have got balls as big as aircraft tyres.' An explanation which the Flight Lieutenant seemed disposed to accept.

The level of trust at times was quite extraordinary. Many of the journalists came to acquire the role of itinerant pedlars in the Middle Ages, always outsiders, tolerated, occasionally useful, but valuable above all as purveyors of scraps of information from the world beyond. Sometimes this led to mutual respect and trust. As I was attached to 2 Para I got to know the then CO, Lieutenant-Colonel H. Jones, well, in the last fortnight of his life. An impetuous, generous and self-doubting man, he used me and my colleague from the *Daily Mail*, David Norris, as his private ear, with no obligations. I remember standing on the roof of the bridge of the ferry *Norland* as it nosed into San Carlos Water past Fanning head for the landing. We were looking through night-vision telescopes to see if there were enemy lights on the foreland. 'How do you think the boys will stand up to it?' we asked. 'I don't know how they'll face being strafed and bombed from the air out in the open' – sharing his innermost worries without a hope of getting any expert advice from us. Once ashore he became impatient as usual. 'We've got to move out, get the thing moving. How can I get in touch with Maggie? We ought to ring Downing Street, tell her to get a grip of her knickers.' Then, waiting at Camilla Creek House the day before the attack on Darwin and Goose Green, the news from his staff that reference had been made on the World Service to the position of his battalion had his mind moving like a whirling dervish. Again a mixture of fun and irony: 'I want to sue John Nott, the Ministry, the Prime Minister, if anyone's killed. Tell Sara she's got to do it. Do you think it's possible, Robert, a manslaughter action?' So it went on for an hour or so; at one point he listed the BBC in his canon of litigants. My misfortune is that I recounted this story two days later to the *Sunday Times,* lately arrived at Goose Green. Later H decided on a letter to *The Times* as the best course. In the evening his 'O', or order group, was calm and precise, fluent and good-humoured, as he addressed his officers behind the yew hedge at Camilla Creek at sunset. Finally he turned to me and said, 'Where do you want to go, Robert? You can come with us or stay behind with the guns, here.' I said I had never been in a thing like this before but wanted to go with the main battle. He replied: 'Neither have I been in a thing like this, and I don't know how I will get on either.'

I subscribe to Wilfred Owen's view that the poetry of war is in the pity of it. The battle of Goose Green was heroic by any standards, because it was the courage of the men and almost nothing else which won the day. The thing I remember most was their companionship, helping the wounded, sorting out the dead, trying to round up prisoners. I cannot pretend these men are angels. In Port Stanley, when the tension of battle was over, the amount of 'proffing' by British troops was considerable – some understandable, some not, such as the thieving of a collection of gold coins from a young vet who had just lost his wife in the final bombardment. They acted like most soldiers in peace as well as war. My perspective as a reporter, I know, was constricted by the enforced, but welcome, companionship of the field, the cold and the miles of marching across peat bog, the occasional shelling and bombing, and the difficulties of communicating with an audience 8000 miles away the colour and circumstances of the rat-pack war.

WINTER WARRIORS

Robert Fox: *The Listener* Thursday 15 July

The success of the Falklands winter campaign by now seems to have been achieved with almost indecent haste. At the time, victory never appeared certain until the surrender was signed. Logistics, weather, disease and resupply seemed to present barriers as forbidding as the craggy mountain features guarding Port Stanley itself. But the fact that the two parachute regiment battalions and the two marine commandos did get to the islands' capital on the evening of 14 June is largely the achievement of an extraordinary partnership between the Force Commander, Major-General Jeremy Moore, OBE, MC and bar, and Brigadier Julian Thompson, OBE. Both Royal Marines, they have known each other for most of their military careers, careers that seem to have reached a natural dramatic climax in the May and June Falklands campaign. Much hard work was done by Fifth Infantry Brigade under Brigadier Tony Wilson, in particular the hard, slogging engagements by the Scots Guards on Mount Tumbledown and the Gurkhas on the morning of 14 June. But the build-up from the first landing at San Carlos to the surrender in Stanley was maintained by Julian Thompson and 3 Commando Brigade.

'It's the bayonets that have done it,' Julian Thompson told me as the fighting was coming to its conclusion. 'That and the artillery and the ability to march across the island and move at night.' He also singled out the success of the Sea Harrier as an interceptor, hitherto almost completely untried in this role, the work of the sappers, signallers and logistics regiments. When he talks about 'the bayonets', he means the fighting men, the infantry on the ground, for whom he still has a strong affection. 'A soldier's soldier' is not an empty cliché applied to the neat and athletic figure of the Brigadier, who looks almost ten years younger than his forty-seven years. Both he and Jeremy Moore, like every senior parachute and marine officer I met in the campaign, look extremely fit, and against the image their corps, 'the bootnecks', once enjoyed, both have more than a touch of the intellectual about them.

Both have been very candid about the risks of the

campaign. Despite the success of the Sea Harrier, the air cover over the ground forces was never anything like adequate. The Harrier patrols at sea, known as the 'cap', could only pick up the enemy aircraft as they were returning from their raids. Lack of air cover was compounded by the disaster of the loss of the *Atlantic Conveyor,* as significant as the loss of the Type 42 destroyers and the Type 21 frigates. The force was already restricted in its helicopter assets, and the loss of three heavy Chinook helicopters and the squadron of Wessex 5s in the *Conveyor* meant virtually all the heavy-lift capability was gone. Much of the force that was to attack Port Stanley would have to march most of the way from San Carlos across East Falkland. The Third Battalion Parachute Regiment and 45 Commando marched all the way.

All this was done in a Falklands winter, one of the mildest on record, it is true. But the Marines, Guards and Paras still had to contend with snowstorms, days of drenching fine rain, trenches that filled up below a depth of two feet, and winds with a chill factor of minus 20 degrees centigrade. On the first night a young Royal Marine of 40 Commando nearly died of hypothermia as he had insisted on staying in a trench filled with three feet of freezing peat-bog water.

In the early days, the biggest hazard was air attack, 'the Farnborough Air Show Days', as they were called at San Carlos. The skill and courage of the Argentine pilots surprised most on the ground there. 'You have to admire them for their skill and courage,' says Jeremy Moore. But why were they so underestimated by some defence specialists writing from London? 'I can't understand it,' says Julian Thompson, 'because if you want the real facts and figures you just have to look at the annual *Military Balance* [published by the International Institute for Strategic Studies]. It shows they had an awful lot to throw at us, particularly Skyhawks.'

Brigadier Thompson says that the campaign became easier to direct as it progressed. The options narrowed and the route was clear. 'We knew we had to end up in Stanley; the question was how?' He adds that some of the plans were like going to London via John o'Groats. One important factor was the training the Argentines had received from the Americans in amphibious warfare. 'Very much the Iwo Jima approach,' explains Thompson. 'You know, up the beach in broad daylight, plenty of noise, fighters roaring overhead.' So he chose to land at night, unopposed and in a secure anchorage, yet not too far from Port Stanley. The final decision was taken with naval and Cabinet approval. Some of the options that emerged from these appear extraordinary. One was a full-out attack on Stanley. In any opposed landing at least thirty per cent casualties can be expected, which would have crippled the ground forces. At the other extreme was the proposal to land on West Falkland and wait for the enemy to attack; Falkland would surely have become another Crimea in that case. Most bizarre of all was the suggestion of landing on Lafonia, the peninsula south of Darwin, miles and miles of open marshland with little cover for ground troops from attacking aircraft and observation posts in the mountains.

Once ashore, the plan was to hold the bridgehead as a logistical base, protected by the 'ring of steel', or the Rapier air-defence missiles. After a week establishing the base, and the loss of HMS *Coventry* and the *Atlantic Conveyor,* the Cabinet demanded action. And action there was at Goose Green. Both General Moore and Brigadier Thompson say that an early victory was needed. 'The achievement of 2 Para was to seek a battle, win convincingly and surprise the enemy,' says General Moore. But no one in London, with the Fleet, at the San Carlos bridgehead, not even the impatient Colonel H. Jones himself, could have known the real risks of that attack. Jones's men of 2 Para were told that they were attacking enemy in company strength, 500 at the most. In the event, there were about three times that number. Only half a battery, three guns, covered the assault, and two mortars. By the afternoon of the action ammunition was running out, and resupply and casualty evacuation by helicopter almost non-existent for two or three vital hours.

The achievement of H. Jones and his men was heroism in battle on the scale of Leonidas and the men of Sparta at Thermopylae. In the afternoon of the battle at the main Battalion HQ the medical orderlies were working with the frenzy of so many sorcerers' apprentices. Steadily mortared and shelled as we crouched by the line of gorse bushes, the only landmark at that point, the unit seemed entirely cut off. All around was the stench of burning gorse and damp peat, the smell of medication for the injured and dying and the sad-faced prisoners, the youngest of them whimpering softly in the cold. At Brigade HQ at San Carlos there was intense anxiety; an anxiety which would be lifted only in the afternoon of the following day when the acting CO of 2 Para, Major Chris Keeble, informed Brigadier Thompson that nearly 1400 Argentine soldiers and airmen had surrendered on the airfield at Goose Green. The day after, Major-General Jeremy Moore flew into San Carlos ahead of 5 Infantry Brigade. 'I had to take the political pressure off Julian's back,' he recalls. 'He was involved in constant referring upwards to all levels in London and to the Fleet. It was his job now to concentrate on the build-up for the attack on Port Stanley.'

The meeting between Jeremy Moore and Julian Thompson in the farmyard at San Carlos, just above the Brigade HQ tents, was the reunion of an old firm. They worked together first when General Moore was commanding the officers' wing at Lympstone and Julian Thompson was chief instructor. One of their first cadets was Rod Bell, now a Royal Marine captain who played a vital role in both the Goose Green and Stanley surrenders. Thompson recalls that because Bell grew up in South America – as a cadet he spoke far better Spanish than English – he was an asset beyond value when it came to acting as General Moore's personal representative to Governor Menendez before the surrender on 14 June.

Jeremy Moore is surprisingly candid about why he became a Royal Marine. At school he wanted to join the Fleet Air Arm, but his housemaster at Cheltenham wrote to his father that 'an ordinary decent plodder like Jeremy' would not make a career naval officer, but he might try the Royal Marines, 'as a last resort'. General Moore, fifty-four this week and retiring from the Corps this month, is the Royal Marines' most decorated serving senior officer. He won the MC in Malaya in 1950, a bar to it in Brunei, and the OBE for Operation Motorman in Northern Ireland. He was due to retire in February this year, but the date of departure was postponed twice. 'Luckily, I gave up the idea of flying with marines pretty soon, otherwise I'd certainly be dead by now.' The first sixteen years with the marines saw active service abroad for nine years, service which he recalls with enthusiasm. Malaya, he says, was an amateur affair compared with the Brunei operation, and later the Borneo confrontation, in which he was first a company commander and then on the divisional staff of Major-General Peter Hunt. 'A marvellous campaign,' he describes it, 'wide-ranging along a border of 1000 miles with the characteristics of each brigade area very different.' It was here that the necessity of a slow, steady build-up came to be appreciated, with emphasis on establishing and supplying artillery as a priority in any move forward; and this was to be repeated in the advance on Port Stanley.

Reflecting on his Northern Ireland service there is more caution. 'It was fascinating. Everybody wants to do it, but you cannot describe it as enjoyable.' The thing he says he learned at the time of Motorman in Derry in 1972 was that the 'military had not got their public relations act together'. He says that Bloody Sunday that year turned out to be 'a stunning propaganda coup for the other side'. For much of that Northern Ireland tour he devoted himself to improving public relations, preparing officers and men for regular television and press interviews. On the Falklands campaign he offers similar criticism: 'The MoD [Ministry of Defence] simply has not got its act together at all on this,' he comments. Earlier in the campaign we had met about a press leak that had eventually reached the BBC World Service which directly involved him. It was revealed by a 'senior MoD official' to the Press Association that General Moore had made a public broadcast appeal for General Menendez and his garrison to surrender forthwith; and this was at least ten days before Stanley fell. In fact General Moore was trying to contact Menendez's staff via the CB radio link used for the islands' health service. The plan was to discuss, first, the safety of the civilians in the capital, and then later establish a means of negotiating surrender; and this project could have been torpedoed by the leak from London.

As these first contacts were being made via Dr Alison Bleaney in Port Stanley, Brigadier Thompson was making preparations for the assault on the capital. 'From the first landing Julian set the pattern with his brigade,' says Moore. 'He is a tremendously professional soldier, with a lot of drive and energy, and is anything but rash. He inspires immense confidence, so all the men did what they did with the same confidence. I was very lucky to have two Parachute Battalions and three Commandos in one brigade. In fact I was lucky, too, to have all eight units, the Scots and Welsh Guards and the Gurkhas.' Both men give the same reasons for the success of the operation. The ability to march over the mountains and attack at night in numbers seems to have surprised the enemy completely. The accuracy of the artillery and the use of naval gunfire were also winning cards. Brigadier Thompson specifically prepared so that three battalions in the mountain engagements could have the support of up to five batteries, though moving them and bringing up 15,000 rounds of ammunition meant days of helicopter flying and some delays to the start of mountain battles.

His description of the last actions on Mount William and Tumbledown and Wireless Ridge is indicative both of the man and his conduct of the winter campaign. I was in the light snow on a forward slope of Two Sisters and saw his helicopter going forward at three in the morning to both battles, displaying still something of the young officer winning the MC in Malaya who had to be restrained by his superiors 'for overdoing things'. He himself recalls: 'The Scots Guards had a bloody hard grind on Tumbledown, but they were still ready to go, being well trained.' He says he remembers how easy it was to handle the men of all units moving forward, and then 'I heard over the radio that the Argentines were all standing up. I told Julian Thompson to go forward. At that moment I had to grab the radio and do it all myself. Harriers were due to drop laser-targeted cluster bombs on Sapper Hill. I was told they could not be recalled as they were less than ten minutes away from target. In fact we stopped them with under three minutes to go.'

Despite the scale of the Argentine collapse, both General Moore and Brigadier Thompson have a healthy respect for the more professional enemy units, particularly the pilots. 'I would say that where the grace of God comes in,' says Moore, 'is that on the first days in San Carlos the pilots went for the escorts and not the amphibious ships, for that might have stopped us altogether.' He says radar skills were excellent, particularly in interception. Technicians were ingenious in improvising such devices as the Exocet missiles on lorries and fixed emplacements at Stanley, one of which hit HMS *Glamorgan* on 12 June. And, concludes Jeremy Moore, 'some of their fighting, particularly by machine-gunners, was very determined in the mountains.' From this there are a number of short-term lessons in the view of Brigadier Thompson, such as the need for lighter, hand-carried anti-aircraft missiles, like the rifle-launched 'stinger', used by the SAS. More secure radio equipment is required in the field, and more night-vision aids. Despite the fact that they thought the British predilection for fighting at night unfair and ungentlemanly, the Argentines appear to have had more night sights and binoculars than the British forces. But Julian Thompson's view of the lessons for the future from the winter war goes beyond particular items of supply, and it has some significance in the light of Mr Nott's latest Defence White Paper. Asked about the decline of amphibious warfare training, he told me: 'It is essential we do not legislate for limited options in the future, for one kind of war in one theatre, such as Europe.'

Both pay compliments to the men serving under them. 'I have been enormously uplifted by them,' says Julian Thompson. 'They are more flexible and more inquiring than they used to be. There are very few old sweats now.' The surprise to me was the extraordinary sensibility and breadth of taste of both these model modern marine commanders. Both are avid students of history, and not just military history. Barbara Tuchman's portrait of four-teenth-century Europe, *A Distant Mirror,* is a favourite with both, and Julian Thompson says he would take up full-time history teaching tomorrow. Jeremy Moore could discuss happily for hours, if he had to leave the service, Tolstoy's portrayal of individuals, the life of Peter Abe-lard, and ballet. Jeremy Moore has a particularly strong religious faith and sums up his attitude to his work in a saying of Dietrich Bonhoeffer: 'Only through discipline can man learn to be free'. Both are without sentimentality.

Jeremy Moore is particularly close to his 11-year-old son, Andrew. Perhaps a letter from young Andrew Moore, never one of the world's great spellers, sums up the apprehension nearly all of us felt in that month of peat, damp, snow, mist, bombs and shells: 'I hope we are going to win, Daddy. I think we will, but I am not shore.'

WELCOME HOME, AND AFTER

Robert Fox: *The Listener* Thursday 22 July

This has been a month of homecomings, and by now nearly all the main elements of the Falklands Task Force have returned. Ferries, helicopter and Harrier squadrons, the Blues and Royals in their light tanks driving up Windsor High Street, the sappers, signallers and Gunners have all had their tales to tell, and rightly have been fêted by their families, friends and country. Most spectacular was the return of the SS *Canberra*, troopship extraordinary, after a voyage which can only be described as epic, 27,000 miles with only one stop. That stop, one of the biggest ironies of the campaign, was at Puerto Madryn in Patagonia, returning 4104 prisoners of war to Argentina. There were no official welcomes and tearful families for those young soldiers. They were shipped off in trucks and coaches to army and air force bases to be 'processed', as the unhappy euphemism has it.

The reception given to the *Canberra* coming up the Channel to Southampton was one of those extraordinary explosions of national feeling which continues to astonish foreign observers about this country. Much of the ceremony was completely unrehearsed; that there was no accident in that streaming flotilla of hundreds of small boats following the liner's rusty white shape round the Isle of Wight still seems a miracle. Despite the thousands of people cheering from the boats and the shore, there was much about the homecoming which was an utterly private experience. With admirable discretion the Prince of Wales visited the ship by helicopter for an hour and a half and then left as she docked at the berth she left at dusk on

Good Friday. Aboard, I found that many of the troops were just beginning to come to terms with the brief but intense experience of the Falklands campaign.

After docking the scene blurred into the private moments of greeting families, friends and well-wishers. Somehow the television and radio commentators, the gaggle of cameramen and technicians, looked outsiders. Much the same happened when the leading elements of the two parachute battalions returned to Brize Norton a few days before *Canberra* made landfall. The official welcome from the generals and Prince of Wales was kept to a minimum, and then the thousands of wives, mothers, fathers and children took their men away. I saw a young doctor, who can only be two or three years from finishing his training, break down in tears greeting his wife and children. I recall the same man six weeks ago, steady as a rock in the dying light by the flaming gorse bushes at Goose Green after tending and operating on the injured and dying for hours under sustained machine-gun and mortar fire.

Most of those arriving at Brize Norton had some indelible memory of the campaign. Lt-Col. David Chaundler of 2 Para recalled the moment before the surrender. 'I saw those Argentines pouring down the hill to Stanley. They were like hundreds and thousands of black ants running back, and then the white flags came up.' 'I remember hearing it was all over, and then my Fire Observation Officer, Mike Pope, threw his arms round me and shouted, "Don't you realise: we're alive. We've made it," ' said Major Martin Osborne, 'C' Company Commander, 3 Para. For RSM Malcolm Simpson the meal he was to have that evening had achieved the mystical and elusive qualities of the Holy Grail. 'It all seems to me to have been days of marching with no rations. One day you had rations and no water, and then you would find you had water and no rations.'

The strange feature of being sent to report both the return of the *Canberra* and the paras at Brize was that, immediately I started interviewing any of the homecoming soldiers, we started talking in almost private code. The other night I met up with four officers of 3 Para and their wives, and two of the crew of the *Canberra*, Helen

128

Hawkett, the accountant, and Lauraine Mulberry, the assistant purser. Much to our wives' bewilderment, and annoyance, I suspect, we began talking again in the currency of the experience we had shared for the past three months. It is not that the images and scenes of the Falklands campaign were any more intense, horrific or unusual than anything experienced in Korea, Vietnam or the Second World War. More people and, in time, whole nations came to share directly or vicariously something of the experience of those campaigns. The outstanding feature of the recent Falklands fighting was that it was such an enclosed affair, remote, private to a few thousand people, and brief. Thus I find that most questions I get about what went on there tend to project the anxieties and attitudes of the questioners more than anything else.

As the immediate tide of emotion at the return of the troops begins to recede, the cooler analysis of the military lessons of the campaign begins. Already defence colleges and staff lecture halls throughout the country are beginning to reverberate to often bitter exchanges about future strategy, the navy arguing for a 'blue water' policy, the army and RAF insisting on the 'Continental commitment', the commitment to Europe. It is reported that the Royal Navy is asking for twelve extra ships to have a capability of global response, a need underlined by the Falklands crisis, while the land strategists reply that the UK's main strategic role will be in the central European sector of NATO. The Navy seems sure not to let the opportunity slip to assert its view, and already the retention of HMS *Invincible* and her two sister ships, the light carriers HMS *Illustrious* and HMS *Ark Royal*, still building, seems to show that the admirals are having some success.

Of all the armed services the Royal Navy is having to do the most radical rethinking of tactical and training policy as well as strategy. In the short winter war the most-quoted military figure was the Duke of Wellington ('A damned close-run thing' and 'Do not congratulate me, Madam, I have lost some of my dearest friends'), followed closely by Admiral Beatty. 'There's something wrong with our bloody ships today, Chatfield,' was one of the most-quoted remarks across San Carlos anchorage. The Royal Navy is fast reassessing construction policy of ships, the strength and quality of armaments and the tactical deployment of anti-aircraft frigates. Editorials in *Jane's Fighting Ships* have lamented for years now that the anti-aircraft frigates have been too lightly armed for self- and fleet-defence, and the pounding these ships took off the Falklands and in Falkland Sound add strength to the argument. Some systems, such as the Sea Wolf missile, were successful, but mounted on the Type 22s such as *Broadsword* and *Brilliant* they appeared capable of defending only the ship they were in, and the guidance computer could become 'confused' if the ship was attacked by low-flying aircraft from several directions. The success of Exocet has been well canvassed, and some counter-measures were established, such as the use of chaff to confuse the guidance mechanism and swinging a ship stem on to the missile's path. One Type 21 frigate is reported to have hit an Exocet with a shell from her 4.5 Mark 8 gun; the missile apparently was guided on to the path of the shells, which were rapid fired. Exocet, in one form or another, has been with the world's navies for some ten years, and it is the next generation of sea-skimming missiles that the Royal Navy will have to start planning against now.

To return to Lord Beatty, the 'something' most wrong with our ships seems to be in basic design. Aluminium superstructures have long been known to burn in intense heat, and this certainly happened with Type 21s like HMS *Antelope* and HMS *Ardent*. Steel ships fared better. HMS *Glamorgan*, a County class destroyer, sustained an Exocet hit from the shore near Port Stanley on the night of 12 June, yet returns to her home port to tell the tale. Cheap PVC-type insulation in the main cable ducts of HMS *Sheffield* was an added hazard as, once alight, it generated clouds of poisonous fumes. According to one report the fires aboard HMS *Sheffield* were made worse by the deep-fry vats in the main galley exploding. Given all these weaknesses, it surprises many ship-design experts that the Government has decided to order the Type 23 frigate as the immediate replacement for those lost or irreparably damaged in the Falklands. Opinion of designers with the Task Force was that the Type 23 design had little merit beyond its cheapness.

Some aspects of ship design worked remarkably well,

and fire-damage procedures promptly acted upon saved a great many lives. On the day the *Galahad* and *Tristram* were bombed, the frigate HMS *Plymouth* sustained at least three direct hits from Mirage attack as she was making her way to San Carlos Water. Her captain, David Pentreith, put fire-damage control drills into action immediately, and two fire-fighting teams flew in from HMS *Fearless*. Smoke was pouring from her stern and her funnel. Yet within an hour all the fires were out, and of her company only one was badly hurt and another slightly injured.

Another success for the navy was the use of naval gunnery, another irony as the Naval Gunfire Support units were due to be closed this year. The 4.5-inch gun of a frigate has the fire-power of one battery of 105mm light-artillery weapons (six guns), and in deterrent as well as destructive power more than proved their worth at South Georgia, Pebble Island, Fanning Head, Darwin, Goose Green and Port Stanley. The other sucesss was machine-guns against low-flying aircraft, and this happened on land as well as at sea. The machine-guns could put up a curtain of fire through which a low-diving aircraft, once committed, would have to pass. This kind of fire gave the Harriers far more trouble than any of the land-based anti-aircraft missiles the Argentines used, such as Roland and the British Tiger Cat. On the land the mere fact that the ground soldiers thought they had something to hit back at the Skyhawks with proved an enormous morale booster. A few days after the landings 2 Para knocked down a pair of Skyhawks as they pulled up over Sussex Mountain, and afterwards just about every man in the battalion told me that he had scored a hit. Judging by the amount of lead that went into the air, he may have been right, too.

The spirit of inquiry is abroad in Argentina, and the Falklands themselves, too. Judging by the mournful faces of many of the prisoners I saw landed at Puerto Madryn, nothing of the inter-service arguments and government inquests in this country can have the bitterness and pathos of what is happening to thousands of those young men now. Two of the prisoners gave me on-the-record interviews about their life as conscripts on the Falklands, interviews in which they wanted to add their gratitude for

131

the way they had been treated as prisoners. 'We have had everything we lacked in six weeks on the hills above Port Stanley,' said one. 'We find the way the British are organised for the prisoners, for peace as well as war, is incredible. Maybe it is the Geneva Convention, but even so it is incredible,' said the other. Both would not allow me to release their names for fear of reprisals against their families. The way the first prisoners were interviewed and processed for information about Geneva Convention violations immediately they got ashore suggested they may not have been too cautious about their anonymity.

Inquiry in the Falklands is more private. First, it takes the form of the question: 'Who knew that the Argentinians were on the point of invasion?' and then: 'Could it have been stopped?' The answer is complicated, but there is no doubt that Buenos Aires was giving the islanders a timetable, demanding serious talks beginning in March on the transfer of sovereignty, or invasion in twelve months. This was certainly mentioned at the New York talks on 27 February, but was not in the Argentinian opening-position paper or the final communiqué. The clue that the threat was serious was given by propaganda broadcasts and government-inspired newspaper editorials almost from the beginning of the year. The radio threats reached a crescendo soon after the New York meeting at which two island councillors, John Cheek and Tim Blake, were present. 'I realise now that they were serious about the timetable. The trouble is that we did not know if the threat was of force being used at the end of twelve months or within that time,' says John Cheek. 'I realise now I got the timing all wrong: I thought an invasion would come in July or August, in our spring, and something must have happened to make them want to move so soon, and the Foreign Office should have had warning of this.' On 9 March Lord Carrington did send a note to Buenos Aires, of which I have seen a copy, which stated firmly that there could be no further talks on the lines agreed in New York 'in the present atmosphere of threats'. 'But you had a new man at the top in Argentina in Leopoldo Galtieri, who took over from General Viola last December,' I submitted to former Governor Rex Hunt, 'and it seemed he was going for a more aggressive foreign policy, and this was read by the commentators quite early?' 'Yes, again, but I didn't think he would be so foolish as to commit the Argentines to armed aggression in the Falklands as he did,' was the reply.

Debates about the future for the Falklanders are more hesitant. It is hard to expand the economy; farming is extremely rough and the boggy terrain and weather are conducive to only the hardiest sheep and small, tough breeds of cattle like Welsh Black. Kelp-harvesting is a capital-intensive but not labour-intensive industry. The only possibilities for expansion are services to the garrison, at least two or three times the native population, and specialist tours for ornithologists. For most of the Kelpers there is no other home to go to. Under the original terms of the British Nationality Bill most were excluded from automatic entry rights to the Unite Kingdom. But their home, what the broadcasting officer in Stanley, Pat Watts, calls 'what used to be our peaceful little islands', is ruined. 'I can't take the kids to the beach here at Stanley any more because of the mines. I used to enjoy going out to my peat bog to cut turf for the fire, of a winter's afternoon. I asked the Royal Engineer officer if it was safe to go back there. He said there were not any minefields marked at the spot on his map. But he said you never knew; and nowhere was safe for miles round Stanley.'

CHRONOLOGY

Friday 2 April	Argentine invasion of Falklands. Royal Marines surrender.
Saturday 3 April	First House of Commons Saturday sitting since Suez. United Nations Security Council passes Resolution 502 calling for an end to hostilities, the withdrawal of Argentine troops, settlement by peaceful means.
Monday 5 April	First Task Force ships, including *Hermes,* sail from Portsmouth. Lord Carrington resigns. Mr Francis Pym becomes Foreign Secretary.
Wednesday 7 April	Britain declares a 200-mile military exclusion zone around the Falklands (effective 12 April).
Thursday 8 April	Mr Alexander Haig, US Secretary of State, arrives in London to begin diplomatic shuffle.
Friday 9 April	*Canberra* sails from Southampton.
Saturday, 10 April	EEC approves trade sanctions against Argentina. Haig in Buenos Aires for talks with Galtieri.
Saturday 17 April	*Canberra* calls at Freetown, Sierra Leone.
Monday 19 April	Haig returns to Washington after breakdown in mediation talks.
Thursday 22 April	Pym flies to Washington.

Friday 23 April	Foreign Office advises British in Argentina to leave.
Sunday 25 April	Britain recaptures South Georgia.
Friday 30 April	US openly sides with Britain after failure of peace efforts.
Saturday 1 May	Harriers and Vulcans attack Port Stanley airfield. Three Argentine aircraft shot down.
Sunday 2 May	Argentine cruiser *General Belgrano* sunk with loss of over 300 lives.
Tuesday 4 May	HMS *Sheffield* hit by Exocet missile with loss of 20 lives.
Friday 7 May	Round of peace talks begins at UN.
Sunday 9 May	Sea and air bombardment of Falklands.
Friday 14 May	Three Argentine Skyhawks shot down.
Saturday 15 May	Marines land on Pebble Island, destroy 11 Argentine aircraft and withdraw.
Thursday 20 May	UN peace efforts break down.
Friday 21 May	British troops establish bridgehead at San Carlos. HMS *Ardent* sunk by air attack. Nine Argentine aircraft shot down.
Sunday 23 May	HMS *Antelope* attacked and sinks after unexploded bomb detonates.
Monday 24 May	Seven Argentine aircraft shot down.
Tuesday 25 May	Loss of HMS *Coventry*. *Atlantic Conveyor* abandoned after being hit by Exocet missile.

Friday 28 May	2nd Battalion, Parachute Regiment, take Darwin and Goose Green. Death of Lt-Col. H. Jones. More air-raids on Port Stanley.
Saturday 29 May	Warships and Harriers bombard Argentine positions.
Tuesday 1 June	Britain repeats ceasefire terms.
Wednesday 2 June	British troops take Mount Kent.
Sunday 6 June	Versailles summit supports British position on Falklands.
Tuesday 8 june	Argentine air attack on landing craft *Sir Galahad* and *Sir Tristram* at Bluff Cove, resulting in the loss of 50 British lives.
Saturday 12 June	Nine killed on HMS *Glamorgan* while supporting advance on Port Stanley.
Sunday 13 June	British forces seize Mount Tumbledown and other key positions.
Monday 14 June	Final stages of battle. White flags raised over Port Stanley.
Tuesday 15 June	Entry of British forces into Port Stanley.

BRIAN HANRAHAN

Brian Hanrahan, who is thirty-three, has been a reporter with BBC TV News for two years. Described by colleagues as 'a quiet, shy and unassuming' reporter he has established a reputation for accuracy and a delightful turn of phrase. Born in Middlesex, he graduated in politics from Essex University and joined the BBC in 1970 as a photographic stills clerk before becoming a scriptwriter and duty editor in the Television Newsroom. His previous assignments have included Northern Ireland. Unmarried, he is a keen amateur actor and regularly appears in amateur dramatic society productions in North London where he lives.

ROBERT FOX

Robert Fox is thirty-seven and joined Radio News in 1974. Since then he has had many foreign assignments, including the Iceland cod war and the recent Italian earthquake. He specialises in Italian affairs and has made many programmes there, particularly on the Red Brigades, and was due to cover the Pope's visit to Britain. Described as 'a slightly donnish, even intellectual figure', he is an Oxford history graduate and joined the BBC in 1968 in the Radio Talks and Documentaries Department. He lives in London with his Dutch wife, Marianne, and their two children, and is a lover of opera as well as being, luckily, a keen sailor.